What a PRODUCER *Does*

What a PRODUCER *Does*

The ART *of* MOVIEMAKING
(Not the Business)

BUCK HOUGHTON

SILMAN-JAMES PRESS
LOS ANGELES

First Edition

Library of Congress Cataloging-in-Publication Data

Houghton, Buck, 1915-
What a producer does: the art of moviemaking (not the business) / by Buck Houghton
p. cm.
1. Motion pictures—Production and direction. I. Title.
PN1995.9.P7H68   1992   791.43'0232—dc20   92-6748

ISBN: 1-879505-05-3

Cover design by Hiedi Frieder

Printed and bound in the United States of America

Silman James Press
1181 Angelo Drive
Beverly Hills, CA 90210

To the memory of Rod Serling—a unique talent.

JUMPING IN

I know that I have opened a can of worms with the word 'Producer' because entertainment entities, both networks and studios, have used the word with such inaccurate profligacy of late that it has lost its power of identification: Associate Producers, Line Producers, Co-Producers, Assistant Producers, Executive Producers! (One can only guess what they all do . . . probably too much or too little.) Some directors have told me that they seldom, if ever, hear from these titular producers. Other directors have told me that their titular producers are constantly and annoyingly in their hair . . . and that the style of producing of which I write is a creative pleasure whenever it occurs.

The controlling executives would be well advised, if they want to be prudent with money and to achieve the best possible cinematic result, to see to it that there is some *one* in that bunch of titles who can do what this book describes . . . alone! There is only *one* function, and to subdivide it is to weaken it. For that vitally necessary person is basically a storyteller who is uniquely armed with a creative understanding of how motion pictures are made in the over-view . . . not a promoter, nor a banker, nor a mechanic, nor a credit hungry writer, and he should be left to do his job without interference from . . . to point out a few more . . . the leading lady's agent, a super production manager, some guy who had a hold on the story property, nor the money man.

It is not vital for the producer to be skillful at 'doing lunch' with powerful agents, nor have an 'in' at Credit

Suisse; nor, necessarily, know how a camera works nor how sound gets onto film—just know how to deal knowledgeably, one on one, with professional people in the art of visual/on-screen storytelling, for the motion picture theater—or for the TV set. The principles are the same for each.

So this book is not about money-raising activities, studio politics, nor the agency circuit (necessary activities, but having little bearing on the job of creatively helping creative forces down the track to the best possible picture); nor will I be writing about technical matters, for there are good manuals and top-level classes covering the minute workings of every motion picture art and craft.

Follows, then, the structure of this book . . . its posture.

As the title promises, I will be writing about the duties of a creative producer, not a businessman. He has an idea and pursues it; or he learns of someone else's idea and seeks the means to realize upon it . . . indeed, to be sure that it is improved upon. A good producer, as an inspirer of creativity, must, himself, be creative.

He is a creative administrator . . . a judge of creativity. He guides and helps hundreds of people toward an objective that becomes increasingly clear-cut as the work proceeds from an idea, through its script and budget preparation, then to shooting (very tense and money hazardous), then to post-production (cost manageable and leisurely if you don't have a pressing air date or release deadline). It's like herding bees with a switch.

He administers everything, but it is not necessary that he be able to write, direct, act, nor compose music in order to help writers, directors, actors, or composers do their best. He knows what good people can do in the important production areas, and presses them to do their best, knowing full well when they are doing less than their best. You don't have to be a chicken to judge the quality of an egg, just a lover of eggs.

He co-ordinates the work of many who may never meet one another until the day when their work comes together, making sure that all hands, however far apart in time or place, serve a common purpose.

He is a majority force in the hiring of every artist who works the picture, being guided by the dictionary definition of that party as "one who professes and practices an art in which conception and execution are governed by imagination and taste." This demands selective creativity from the producer.

He is the center to whom everyone turns with their complaints, their questions, their grievances. Diplomacy!

He is the quietest man in the operation because, if he has performed his role well, there's nothing to shout about. Story, management, performance, money . . . all under well-thought-out control. Heaven!

His agenda, or syllabus, is the budget. Therein, awaiting dollar entries, are dozens of items that also define a separate creative function that must be manned, administered, and brought off to the greatest possible perfection. Story, direction, cast, etc., etc., etc.,

Let us allow those items to be my chapter headings.

Table of Contents
PRODUCTION BUDGET

1
THE STORY

The basis from which all else about a movie springs. As a producer you get stories on your desk by broadcasting your needs to the community—agents, friends who write, strangers who have shown skills in your area of interest, and idle writers who accept your invitation to a screening of the pilot (if you are in television). If you are in funds, you also have a Story Editor who pumps up his friends, reads the appropriate magazines, keeps his library card active, and sends his findings to you. If you have a big studio attachment, there's an expensive staff of readers who sift through everything that's printed against long odds of finding anything worth dramatic adaptation, and they broadcast their findings, good and bad, throughout the studio.

The story will come to you in many forms: novels, short stories, stageplays, screenplays, treatments, thumbnail sketches, verbal pitches across your desk, an idea of your own.

Now you have to judge what's been put before you. You must know exactly what you are looking for. In whichever producer role you find yourself—television or theatrical features—you must narrow your mind to focus on exactly what the ground rules are under which you are operating; develop a precise set of standards that will measure a story's fit to your needs. There can be fateful repercussions all down the production line if any of those standards are ignored. And you save valuable time if you have guide lines to make yourself quickly discard unsuitable material.

I am speaking of story elements that are solely on the producer's back . . . not the "givens" for any good story . . . such as an appealing theme, good conflicts, attractive lead and subsidiary characters, compelling settings, provocative plot, strong and solid emotional elements; these are basic. The producer, naturally, thinks of these as he reads, but then he must watch for many other things that may slip through everyone else's fingers.

Seven guidelines to the *movie* story:

1. First, and most importantly, keep firmly in mind the peculiar needs of drama which no other form of story-telling must obey: open conflict. Jack Woodford, dead and gone (saying much the same thing as Aeschylus, also dead and gone), put it well in his book, *Plotting*: the curtains do not really open on a drama until the leading character finds someone or something standing in the way of his wishes or drives (it may be a girl who is hard to meet or a bank that is hard to get into); the drama progresses only while that character (our hero) makes successive attempts to overcome that obstacle (the heavy); it only truly grips an audience when something or someone (the personification of something) seems about to thwart the lead character's efforts; and it all comes to a climax time, the Second Act curtain (to use an applicable stage term), when the opponents are in deadly deadlock.

2. Cost. Yes, even Steven Spielberg watches the bucks. This takes some understanding of budget matters which I will take up in Chapter Six.

3. In reading novels and short stories, be wary of the story that charms but will be hard, or impossible, to dramatize because it carries you along on internal struggles and conflicts that resist being brought out into that openness demanded for a dramatic scene. Some novelists are fine story tellers, but their work is hard to adapt to a dramatic form; their novels are about people's insides, the withholding of which from public view is part of their technique. Point: don't invest in rights and a writer's services if dramatization . . . the codeword . . . is a major hurdle to conveying the story's values.

4. Again, about putting money into a novel and into screenwriting costs: it risks waste if the dramatic need for "economy of attention" is neither observed nor needed in the novel. A good novel can be spread out every which way, undigested; but a movie must be compact, even if it is lightweight . . . every scene pertinent to what went before and driving interest onward. Speaking of compaction, read *Doctor Zhivago*, then see the picture. What a masterful, mind-boggling job Robert Bolt had to perform in defying this dictum of mine . . . turn the rambling complexities of the Russian Revolution with a nice little love story running through it into a compelling love story against the background of the Russian Revolution. Avoid this sort of challenge unless you like doing the near-impossible.

5. Try hard to make your story (let's say you're now enthused about one) pass the test of

being universal in its appeal. There are some very specialized theatrical films of narrow or cultural purpose that I would have been proud to have produced, but I would have made sure that the money people knew that they would have a very tough time getting their costs back . . . and probably wouldn't. Successful film, artistically and/or financially, must appeal to a broad segment of the world's public. Yes, cost retrieval now is world-dependent. And that means that universality's only common denominator is human nature itself . . . not just college kids, not just baseball fans, not just old, young, male, female, etc. What sort of story appeals to the human side of most everyone . . . everywhere? I believe that it is one that lies within the bounds of our common experience, that affirms the human condition (be it via laughter or by way of tragedy) and proves, as Faulkner put it, that "Man will prevail."

6.   Watch for silk among the shoddy. Often there is a wonderful story, right down your alley, that is wretchedly written. Plow in, but don't hire the author to do the screenplay.

7.   In movies, be they for the theater or TV, rememberthat you are ultimately facing an audience with few preconceptions about your picture other than what the title has suggested, the generally distrusted hints in the ads, and sometimes the star. Sitting on their respective tokuses, they are saying, "What you got? Let's go." They'll be patient for a while. Get started early! Some stories, inherently, take forever to get going.

How does this story search process start up? Where do you begin? Nowadays, very few producers are on salary to a studio or a production organization. Most are independents who develop material out of their own thought processes, their own reading, their agent's hustle . . . with their own money, or money borrowed, or writers wangled into writing a screenplay for no money until the slow process of production starts (in the latter case, by Writers Guild rules, the screenplay belongs to the writer, with only a moral obligation tying him to the producer's plans).

Some producers have "first look" arrangements with a "producing company" entity under which they are obligated to show first to that management team whatever they discover or develop, before taking it elsewhere. For this, they have an inside track for a story development loan and are provided with a secretary, sometimes studio services (like the Story Department), an office, and the status that all that brings.

This area is mainly promotional work . . . in-fighting with agents and production heads . . . during which you are almost bound to lose if you are small, relatively new, or under-financed. The publishers send their hot galleys, and the agents send their new scripts, to the prospect who will pay the most: the major studios . . . then the major independents, then it will filter down to the smaller bankrolls.

It's a power game between the agent who must cement the loyalty of pricey clients with "top dollar" when the time comes, and the top buyers who won't hold their jobs for long if the best properties sail by them.

"Naomi's got a good one in the computer . . ." slyly said.

"When can I see it?" anxiously said.

"Well, y'know, I gotta play fair with Naomi." Butter would melt.

Wounded feelings. "You promised . . ."

"Now you know I like to do business with you. Let me see what I can do . . . couple weeks, outside."

Several elegant social occasions and a few lunches later (if you're up for playing the game this way), this agent hands Ms. Naomi's script to the top ten buyers simultaneously. (With any luck, you are one of them.)

"Sorry, but Naomi insisted." She probably didn't.

This story search is a tough one, for over and above the normal good-sense standards of looking for sound dramatic material, there are the diplomacies mentioned above and other standards peculiar to the picture industry. Such as:

1. Statistical standards. What sort of subject matter is hot now (determined by box-office reports) and, if you find one like it, can you get it into the theaters before the trend runs out? Market trends are studied and studied for firm clues, with much the same result as studying American newspapers with a view to guessing trends in today's Russia.

2. Star hunger. Are you seeking to fill a gap in a bankable star's schedule? What is that player best in? Does he/she know what he/she's best in?

3. A type of historically dependable popular picture. High adventure involving special effects like no one has ever seen before? A romantic comedy with a "boy meets girl" opening unlike any ever seen before? Street-level adventure with a new cause for violence? Racism, drugs, the stock market, Congress . . . something in the social significance department?

4. Suiting your financier or studio boss. They all have their favorite sort of picture, and it is well to know what that leaning is . . . for it will

often overcome statistics, freshness, star appeal.

There's another possibility within the producer function that some pursue successfully and others have no taste nor talent for. And that is originating an idea, finding a writer who responds, and getting it scripted . . . with one's own money (a very questionable practice; don't invest anything but your time in this hazardous business) . . . borrowed money . . . or by inducing the writer to write it for no cash up front and a premium price in prospect if it all works out (really against Writers Guild rules, but, in a practical world, often done.)

In the absence of anything exciting on your desk or a paying contract, staring out the window in search of an idea to start up this process is often well worth it . . . even if you only come up with a gimmick (let's do Captain Nemo as of the year 2010 with a space ship), or think up a springboard (the rascally black sheep in a rich family inherits all the money), or rediscover an old novel (Zola's *L'Argent*), or dig up an old and successful movie (*Greed*, based on the Norris novel *McTeague*, and made in '23 by Von Stroheim). Alice Kahn's funny column offers some classics you can steal from. [See page 8.]

A high-risk fact that feature entrepreneurship must face is that no studio, no organization, *has* to make x-number of pictures per year. Sure, they have to make some, but one like *Home Alone* or *Dances with Wolves* will keep their exhibitors happy for the better part of the year. Then they fill in with a few other in-house productions and negative pickups (pictures other companies without exhibition ties made on the speculation that they would somehow find an exhibitor). Consequently, there is not a consistent demand like there is in television or cable. Ergo: if you find yourself without a job, speculate on finding a story that television or

In one of Alice Kahn's columns, she noted that Eddie Murphy was developing a script based on Dante's *Inferno*. Ms. Kahn proceeded to demonstrate that other scripts could be developed from the same resources. Like:

FAUST	Guy closes merger with the devil. Seems to be surviving at the top. Runs into trouble.
THE SCARLET LETTER	Frustrated housewife has affair with town priest. Starts sartorial trend.
HAMLET	New-age wimp tries to avenge death of dad. Drives girlfriend nuts. Cuts self on poisoned blade. Can't do anything right.
JANE EYRE	Au pair takes job in weird household. Finds the wife in a closet. Has affair with the hubby.
CATCHER IN THE RYE	Disturbed teenager launches anti-graffiti campaign.
PARADISE LOST	Hell-raiser rebels against Big Guy. As a result, couple gets evicted from home.
DON QUIXOTE	Guy attacks alternative energy development.
GREAT GATSBY	Guy overinvests in real estate to impress Jodi Foster lookalike.
PRIDE AND PREJUDICE	Bitchy woman goes after clever guy, ends up with rich guy. Decides that's clever.
ROBINSON CRUSOE	Stuck on a desert island in the days before NEA funding, guy has homoerotic experience.
CRIME AND PUNISHMENT	Student kills neighbor. Gets caught by detective with hemorrhoids. Has religious experience.
ODYSSEY	Bummed out by war, hero sails around the world. Wife sets new Guinness record for fidelity.
OEDIPUS REX	Man Falls for older woman. Freaks when she turns out to be his mother.
LOLITA	Distinguished professor debauches child. Tours America. Kills critic.

cable will like; their appetite is steady, voracious, and less persnickety about stars.

The mind-set you bring to the episodic television story-search must encompass some added considerations over and above what has been discussed for theatrical drama.

In television: first, and most difficult, is the story for the pilot script, which, in turn, may become the pilot picture. Whether you work for the network, or the cable company, or on your own, you are trying to catch executive attention . . . and the birth of a series is one of the most wasteful ways known to man of winding up with an end product that finally sees the light of day. The window of opportunity? Twenty-one hours per network per week to fill with enter-tainment—comedy, melodrama, action-adventure, law, medicine, police . . . the mix . . . that's your market. And a discouraging target it is. Literally thousands of proposals will be made by ambitious producers/entrepreneurs; only hundreds will be financed for a pilot script; only dozens will be ordered into pilot; only eight or ten of those dozens will go on the air as tentative series; only three of those will survive into a second season!

I have never struggled in this promotional arena because the odds against making a living in it, or enjoying it, are unfavorable for me. Also, what I know how to do is generally inapplicable until a pilot film is ordered. Up until that moment, many man hours will have been devoted to audience surveys; program analysis of a network's impact, area by area, (rural/big city, east/west); then subject spread (sitcoms/police/soaps/medical/legal); and then the same study is done on the other networks for comparative purposes. There are soon executive decisions about how a submission fits those statistical criteria: "Are we short on comedy?" "Is the audience ready for another medical show?" "Will this star name draw enough to get this thing started?" This is important work, but not producer's work. I have produced six pilots, four of which went on into series, and, in each case, I was handed a script that had been developed by a combination of studio and network creative machinery plus a writer, whose idea it might have been, but whose scripting was done in conformity to the network objectives: "plenty of action"— "physical comedy"—"tough talk"—"sly"—etc.

At that point, having been hired to produce the script in the best manner and in the style indicated, I proceeded to follow the principles that I will be outlining in subsequent chapters as to the choice of a director, casting, etc.

The pilot, and the first few episodes, shape the series. You are beginning to learn what works and what does not . . . the type of story . . . the unique skills of the star and the major supporting players.

"The Twilight Zone" was shaped by Rod Serling. In his first few scripts his instincts led him to a pattern that he and I soon agreed upon as the bottom-line basis for buying stories for adaptation and for his own originals. That pattern became the rigid standard by which I did my judgmental work on story submittals. You must discover your pattern and use it to judge story usefulness.

"The Twilight Zone" pattern:

Find an interesting character, or a group, at a moment of crisis in life, and get there quickly; then lay on some magic.

That magic must be devilishly appropriate and capable of providing a whip-lash kickback at the tag.

The character(s) must be ordinary and average and modern, and the problem facing him (her, them) must be commonplace. ("The Twilight Zone" always struck people as identifiable as to whom it was about, and the story hang-ups as resonant of their own fears, dreams, wishes.)

Allow only one miracle or special talent or imaginative circumstance per episode. More than one and the audience grows impatient with your calls on their credulity.

The story must be impossible in the real world. A request at some point to suspend disbelief is a trademark of the series. (I can think of only three shows that *could* have happened.)

Mere scare tactics will not fill the bill.

A clever bit of advanced scientific hardware is not enough to support a story. "The Twilight Zone" was not a sci-fi show.

With ground-rules this precise, Rod and I and our story editor could get through the material that came our way quickly and accurately. Most of the printed material in the field was science fiction, depending on hardware and futurism—which was often damn fine reading, but not for "Twilight Zone" adaptation. As it finally turned out, I bought nineteen stories for Serling to adapt, and thirty-three for others to screenplay (Serling wrote forty-nine originals in those first three seasons). Then I was ready for the next step: the writer, which I take up in the next chapter.

But first, the producer's story search problems should be examined as they must be handled in other types of television shows, like situation comedies, police stories, etc. The pattern, as developed by each show's pilot and first few exposures to the public, should try to be as distinctive as possible. Yet they're often much alike because a show has to appeal to a huge audience of all types, ages, degrees of prosperity, living circumstances (be it big city, farm, or desert) if it is to pay its way; and the common denominators— the dramatic or comic skewers—that will pin that huge cross-section to the TV screen are few. We're back to "universality" as discussed a few pages ago, but it applies much more severely to television than to motion picture marketing. A fair generalization: in order to succeed, a television program needs twice as many viewers than a motion picture needs ticket buyers.

Therefore the problems, the springboards, the events that provide the core or theme for a television episode's story are often commonplace . . . taken out of the newspaper . . . out of yesterday's quarrel with the producer's neighbor, etc. The producer's main concern is to question just how interesting it will be to watch as his leading man, his family, his office group, this klatch of women, deal with that particular problem. You can be sure that The Fat Man and Hunter have both been faced with the same opening-of-story: "The bank has been robbed!" Or Nurse Jones runs into the hospital corridor in the first thirty seconds of air time with "Please come to Room 22 right away . . . the patient is fibrillating" (or some such compelling word). Or mother learns that fifteen-year-old Janice has birth control pills in her purse. It is the star's unique way (stemming most often from the "star persona") of dealing with this problem or that one which becomes the story's come-on for the producer . . . and he grabs it when it's a fit. Equally, some commonplace problems of humanity will not play well for the star, and the story is rejected.

There are other guidelines peculiar to each show. And knowing that peculiarity is very important if you wish to stay on the air: it is your show's franchise to public approval. "Colombo" has to have a yarn where you can show the crime being performed at the outset . . . and still remain interesting while Colombo slowly, painfully unravels it. "L.A. Law" needs to find three or four relatively small legal or personal problems that will meld together spaghetti-like; this series is generally several short stories per episode. So is "Murphy Brown," with a bagful of news-gathering problems per week.

Know what makes your show work! I produced a Family-In-The-West show once; it was very successful and almost always depended on a frontier-type crisis that drew the violently divergent members of the family together for a fight. I produced an anthology hour some years back in which each show was cast from the same group of players . . . a repertory company; I am sure that a large measure of its appeal to a good year of audiences was the curiosity . . . the foretaste . . . about what one of the company who played a bit part tonight would be like when he did the lead in a show down the line. The need for a strong story to suit the particular talents of each one of those ten players guided our story search.

The producer of a television series must obey one other insistent demand: the story must start quickly. If you don't grab interest in the first few minutes, the remote controls start twitching. That is why so many legal, medical, and law-enforcement shows are on the air and always have been: there is immediate and dramatically provocative crisis-involvement inherent in these professions. Not so with a plumber nor a gardener nor a philosopher.

For practice, watch three or four episodes of one successful show, making notes as to what factors each of the episodes have in common. Look beneath the skin! For these elements are not obvious: Cosby is always in love with his family, but you get that indirectly as a feeling, even when he's angry; he never says, "I love you all." Watch how "Golden Girls" divide up the screen time between the starring women. (I realize those shows won't be on the air when you read this; "life expectancy" for a hit is five years.)

The producer of long-form movies, be they for cable or a network, obeys the same guidelines as a producer for the movie house.

The seven special story guidelines to watch for as you read (which I covered on pages 2-4) hold firm, but the television principles that followed do not . . . unless you are making a sequel, in which case, as in television, you will be inspecting any proposed story carefully, demanding those elements that worked before.

So much for what thoughtful technique or statistical data/science can be applied to story hunting . . . which is damn little, I confess. Perhaps it is all visceral, as a studio boss character in one of Ben Hecht's short stories says: "Don't argue with me. I know what's right in my gut. When I cry over something, the world will cry. When I laugh, the world slaps its knees. When I get scared, the world gets goose-flesh, That's how I pick 'em: by my gut."

2
THE WRITER AND
THE SCREENPLAY

Now comes the problem of selecting the first, and perhaps the most important, member of the picture's creative team . . . and then the task of guiding your choice wisely. No matter how well the work is done down the production line, a picture can fail if the screenplay has not been crafted properly. If it's staccato action/adventure, it still won't be crisp if the succession of plot scenes are languid; if it's yuppie/high finance with the razor blades just barely concealed, it won't chill the audience unless the dialogue is smart-ass cruel. In short, I have seen pictures that fall far below the script's promise, but I haven't ever heard of a fine picture based on a poor script.

The producer has a two-pronged task: what needs doing and who should do it?

What needs doing, of course, depends entirely on the story form you start with. The task is the same, be it comedy, melodrama, sci-fi, etc.

1. Say you've got a story springboard, or a theme, or a mere idea . . . sometimes not even on paper. Complete development and fleshing

out is the challenge; so a strong constructionist is required first . . . one who knows how to build a solid framework on which emotions can hurtle upwards and events can succeed each other with cumulative impact. Then comes a dialogue expert who, luck permitting, will be the same screenwriter.

2. Or, you've got a fine story from another medium . . . short story, stage play, novel . . . needing adaptation and/or dramatization. Some adaptations are easy; I call them writing a screenplay with a pair of scissors. Some others are a study in deletion and condensation. And some are a full job of reconstruction: the thrust, the story, and the characters are all there, but not organized to meet the rising needs of a drama. What's needed here most often is a good, sound, experienced pro . . . maybe even a mechanic in his automatic thinking and way of working. You are not looking for inspirational flights; you are looking to re-package good material along expert cinematic lines.

3. Sometimes you have a full story outline . . . a step-by-step construction in terse, complete sentences . . . perhaps one submitted by a writer or one that you worked out cooperatively with a writer as a proposal for financing the full screenplay. Construction in hand, you must hope that writer is agile in dialogue and brisk with plotting.

4. Finally, there is the situation wherein you have a script on your desk (however it got there—assigned to you as employee, an in-house development, newly bought, agent submitted) that needs repair on one, two, or all

three of the following grounds.

a) A first problem may be that this script (good enough to be bought) is not fully realized. It's excellent plot line leads to action, but that action is not explosive, nor fresh, nor chilling. Or it has some of the most imaginative, bang-bang, and frightening action sequences that you've ever heard of or seen, but the emotional motivation for their occurrence is weak. Or it's a fine love story with a fresh, merry pattern through the boy-meets-girl/boy-gets-her-back drill, but there is not one moment of the tenderness . . . the touch of sentimental magic . . . that seals a love story right into audience's hearts. Or it's one charming, witty, feisty scene after another without a shred of plot with which to maintain attentive interest (people will not sit still for 90 to 120 minutes of unrelated jokes and badinage, however good— ask any stand-up comic). Out of your own experience in the movie house and at home on TV, you can recite the numerous flaws that should have been recognized and dealt with before getting up on the screen. Which is to say that the problems that need addressing are not always evident except to those with hindsight (you in the theater or on the couch) or by use of a very perceptive crystal ball (you as producer). Well, polish your crystal ball and show it to the writer. Now, the only way for that crystal ball to stay clear and useful is to keep your checklists (you got them from writing classes, personal observation, or dreadful mistakes made in the past that enhance your "experience table") on your desk top and use them as a template against the present script.

b) A second common problem is that shooting this script will cost too much. The producer sights this problem in one of two ways: the production manager has just completed the picture budget, and it is too high (more about how this is calculated and the standards by which it is judged in Chapter Six), or certain scenes are spotted whose inherent costs are out of proportion to their value in advancing the story or entertaining the audience. Example: a car smashes into a bus, which causes a traffic tie-up, thus bringing Jane's and Carl's car windows into a side-by-side confrontation and Jane can tell Carl that their appointment with the President is off until Tuesday; a twenty second scene, accomplishing little that could not be told more simply, and costing a day's shooting. (In high-cost, action/adventure, logic-be-damned pictures, this way of conveying simple information would be cherished.)

The budget will reveal other high points of cost, some of which you lower realistically, some you eliminate, and some you leave alone. Don't economize on the heart of the picture: there's a wisdom in knowing when to scrimp a hundred dollars and when to lavish a hundred thousand . . . the first is an unimportant element, the second is a vital element. There's a wisdom also in not cutting budget allowances that you know very well are going to cost just that much when the time comes to do that work; you are lying to yourself and others if you cut dollars out of the post-production sound budget on the premise that you are going to dub the picture in record time.

c) Thirdly, even in a fine script, you might have to alter a few things, maybe many things, in order to interest the star(s) who will support your budget. If it's only a matter of dialogue, then you and a writer study that star's last two or three pictures, looking for habits of speaking and mannerisms that are a part of his stardom. Sam is a man of few words; Ed's loquacity is his main charm; Audrey is an innocent who has to struggle for the right words in a tough situation; Jim is a sophisticate whose vocabulary is pointed and at his beck and call. Etc. Then too, there is the challenge of fleshing out the leading role so that the star will occupy more space; give scenes formerly handled by the second lead to the star; write in scenes that were formerly thought unnecessary to the story's progress . . . which may be fine now that they are in a star performer's hands. Indulge in a little flattery: change the title from *Stardust* to *A Man Alone* . . . or *A Woman Knows*.

Story balance? There is a graphic, visual way to view this that is sometimes informative about dramatic balance and answers such questions as: Is the leading character occasionally out of the script for too long a time? Is the sub-plot up front too often or too lengthily? etc. [See page 20 for sample.] Thusly, take any sort of graph paper with both vertical and horizontal lines regularly spaced: along the top of the sheet horizontally assign a script page number to each vertical column; then, along the left side, assign a broad horizontal space to all items of interest to you—the cast, one by one—the bank robbery plot—the love story—talk scenes—action scenes—musical numbers—whatever is a real factor in the entertainment. Then, with marker pens

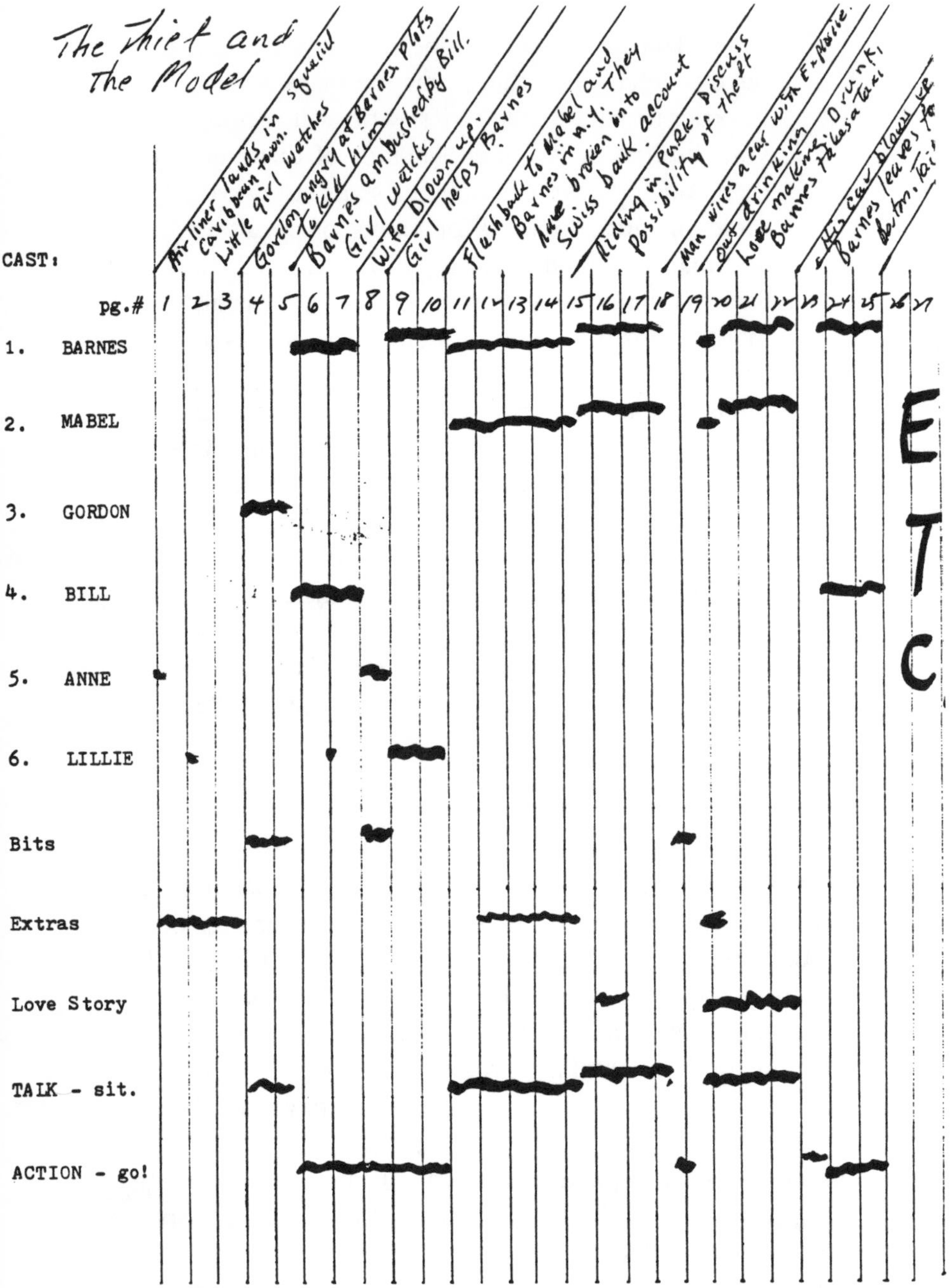

The Thief and The Model

Column headings (diagonal, left to right):

- Airliner lands in Cavio brun town. Little girl watches
- Gordon angry at Barnes. Plots to kill him.
- Barnes ambushed by Bill.
- Girl watches
- Wife blown up.
- Girl helps Barnes
- Flashback to Mabel and Barnes in n.y. They have broken into Swiss bank account
- Riding in Park. Discuss possibility of theft
- Man wires a car with E-Mobile.
- Quit drinking. Love making. Barnes takes a Taxi
- Drunk.
- History draws up. Barnes leaves the botm. Taxi

CAST:

pg.# 1 2 3 4 5 6 7 8 9 10 11 12 13 14 15 16 17 18 19 20 21 22 23 24 25 26 27

1. BARNES

2. MABEL

3. GORDON

4. BILL

5. ANNE

6. LILLIE

Bits

Extras

Love Story

TALK - sit.

ACTION - go!

E T C

run lines under the page numbers on which the horizontal factors occur. Barnes appears with Bill (plus a short appearance by Lillie) in an action-filled scene from page 5½ through 7: four wavy horizontal lines, going from the middle of column 5 on to 7, beside Barnes' name, beside Bills' name, beside Lillie's name, and beside the "Action - go!" line, graph these appearances. Then, to study this graphic interpretation of your picture, draw lines at a forty-five-degree angle above the page numbers wherein the scene begins and ends, and within the margins thus created, write a short description of the scene: "Barnes ambushed by Bill. Girl watches." You can thus study each element in your script quantitatively and metrically. I have done this often without any particular objective in view, and found that, indeed, one element was not on screen often enough . . . another was up front much too often. Etc.

Now that you've settled on what needs doing, comes the "Who should do it?"

Put your heart in your mouth and start surveying the writers you know, have heard of, read. And be sure to realize that you are on a most important mission. Like many of the other artists and craftsmen whom you will be selecting from the industry's rich inventory, there may be only a five percent or ten percent difference between any two of them . . . but that small difference is eminently worth having in your favor. Good pictures (and no one sets out to do any other) are much dependent on small details . . . little dots of emotional effect . . . of acute observation subconsciously absorbed in the theater . . . of atmosphere (created by words, images, colors, sounds) supporting the story; so you must struggle for that five to ten percent edge in your choices.

Of course, writers come in all sizes, shapes, and distinctions as to their particular skills. In general, most screenplay writers with an experience record can do most everything needed; but, like all humans, each one has peculiarities and differences in taste and expertise that make him/her distinctly better at one kind of job than another.

In making your choice of writer, you will be looking to avoid little weaknesses and grab onto little strengths . . . according to the needs of the material. How do you train your selectivity? Here are a few clues.

For instance, there are some writers who simply cannot revise or adapt the work of others. They are uncomfortable with other ideas or ways of doing things. They have to start from scratch for their engine to work. It's not snobbishness nor self-pride; a minimal comparison would be your personal route from your home to the beach—it's hard to get yourself to drive another way. As many times as a "Twilight Zone" script needed a little tinkering, Serling couldn't get down to a polish. "But, Buck, I'd never have started the story where Sam did. So how can I fix page sixteen?"

You can detect this mentality from your first chat with a prospect; he wants to start from scratch. You have to be watchful for this hang-up when the task before you is adaptation or polish . . . when you like, in the main, what you've got, but your need is to improve or revise, not start over.

Then there are some writers who cannot endure; their span of productive concentration will not carry them onto the long trail that gets to the end of Act II or the beginning of Act III. This is immaterial in half-hour or even hour TV, but it is a back-breaker in the full span of a theatrical motion picture when audience patience traditionally and dependably ends at about seventy to eighty minutes and they are, collectively, saying, "What else you got?" or "We've been sitting still here for a hell of a long time." This writer's lack of endurance is not a matter of talent nor time spent. It is only that the long form demands a concentration on a set of characters and a set of situations through mounting complexities that are long past some writers capacity to stay fresh and dynamic. It is a matter of attention span; some people cannot read a long book. This endurance factor inhibits the range of many highly successful television writers whose writing habits and skills were shaped to meet the needs of the shorter form . . . the speed often required, the hard-hit-and-get-away of a medium that interrupts its story telling for ads. I know many good TV writers who had a hard time when they got a theatrical motion picture assignment or even a Movie-for-TV. They're sprinters, not long distance runners.

There's another sort of writer, and damn good if on the right assignment. The adapter. He cannot originate! Given a good western to convert into a modern cop drama—or a strong outline—or a fine script to polish for one reason or the other, or an adaptation from another medium, this one will proceed to do an above average job. But don't pull such a one into the office to look over a bare idea . . . a springboard. You can generally identify these writers by their credits; they are always joint screenplays or adaptations of fine basic material. Incidentally, don't knock this band of writers; when you need one of them, he will do far better for you than a more imaginative writer who is inclined to get off the good track onto some notion of his own.

So far I've dealt with the holes in some writers' talents which you must be wary of. Now to the skills which you must look for when it becomes clear that you need this type and not that type. (Meanwhile, remembering that most of them who are worthy of your attention at all are damn good . . . ranging from plodders to sky-rockets). You're just looking for that personal peculiarity, that bump of strength that gives THIS writer an edge for doing THIS writing job in the best possible way.

First and foremost is the writer with a talent for dramatic construction—the classic constructionist—understanding the sub-structure necessary to a film; like the steel frame to a tall building, you never see it, but the building doesn't stand without it. The work generally results in a 'no-word-wasted' outline which proves that you can get to a good Act I curtain from THIS start, and that the ingredients are in hand for proceeding to an Act II curtain of great tension and forward thrust, and that the ending in mind from the beginning will fall into place re-soundingly. (I use the words Act and curtain as if I came from the theater; I do not, but, believe me, the stairway upward by which audience interest progresses, and the stairway's sudden changes in direction by which an audience gets excited, are the same in both media; it's drama in either case). This writer's outline will probably be without color or nuance or, generally, characterization. Bare bones. Scene by scene. Then that writer is ready for the screenplay which, at minimum, will be soundly built, ready for embellishments at someone else's hands if this first writer is not skilled there. This is the constructionist who was mentioned as vital to the producer who is setting sail with only an idea, or just a theme, or a story springboard.

There is another sort of writer who has an edge over others in certain areas. Experienced, technically skilled ,a professional mechanic; does good "B" work, and the resulting screenplay will seldom hit the jackpot, but it will usually get into easy shooting range of the jackpot. A plodder. But when you're pursuing an idea, a one-liner, or even adapting something from another medium, this tedious spadework usually has to be done in order to test the various steps toward solution through a patient mind . . . one who is in no hurry (usually a nine-to-five worker) . . . one who has seen and retained in memory most of the dramatic devices known to the profession . . . and one who is not thrown off a single-minded approach to the task by a rush of wild-hair ideas. You get three pages of script per day, but it's steady on track. Now, this writer may be the one . . . or you may have to dig up someone else . . . to put icing on the cake, but the cake is there to put icing on; that's the point.

"Gusher" is the word I use to describe some of the creative artists any producer runs into; indeed, often tries to find. They spout out ideas in a torrent of creativity, without second thoughts, nor editing. They are imaginative, free spirits with churning, agile minds. Their script work will be far too long, and probably contain plot devices that are mutually contradictory. (This latter situation occurs, not because they are stupid, but because they are pursuing a runaway course that they think is quite good and there's no time to go back to make corrections.) There will be far too many pages and too many ideas, but if you will shop among this outpouring with the same care that you would when shopping for homogeneity (not necessarily similarity) at Van Cleef & Arpels, you might very well find the same quality gems. The other, dark side of this writer's coin is that the script will be unusable; on the way

to Valhalla, the work got diverted to the River Styx
. . . muddy and murky.

Quite often, you can use a "gusher" to great
advantage when you are seeking improvements in
the dialogue, either in trying to tailor matters to a
performer or to enrich a character. The gusher will
help you, out of his fertility, to find wonderfully
new ways to say old things. It may be on the
twentieth try, but many a writer doesn't have twenty
variations stored up in his mind for . . . well, "I love
you" for example. Or, "You are a no-good S.O.B.!"

The prize in this search is the "old China hand,"
the intuitive story teller, basically extroverted and
therefore especially observant of people and their
behavior, who, after years of productive dramatic
experience, going back to radio, perhaps, is almost
infallible. With unerring instinct he goes to the
problems that we have been discussing, and applies
the techniques that we have been discussing. His
output will always be worthwhile, if . . . and here's
the problem . . . if he takes the job; for out of his
professionalism and instinct, he knows what he
cannot do. This writer is intuitive; at a cocktail party,
he tells a "nothing" story and it gets a big response.
And he applies these instincts to his writing. The
producer will not have to "discover" this writer, nor
find him under a rock; he will be well known in the
community, generally busy, and selective. Such
writers have noticeable strengths as to the type of
material they like and do best . . . comedy, melodrama, whatever. As you get acquainted with your
material and find a fit, you must remember this man
and try to get him if you can.

Now then, there are a few writer types that the producer must avoid: the novice and the talker. Unfortunately, it takes money and patience to teach motion picture methods to ambitious beginners, be they journalists, poets, or just the movie-struck. They come cheap; so buy an idea from a newcomer if you must and nurse him along through outline and even screenplay, but it will be slow and frustrating. I have done this on a few occasions, whether out of shortness of budget or good will, I forget, but it was a mixed bag . . . one went on to great success and one, I remember well, sold his word processor. Of course, there are so many books on screenwriting now, and courses offered, that the incidence of a true newcomer to screenwriting may be rare these days.

The "talker" is a phenomenon that anyone in sales will recognize: he can sell anything, reducing his victim to an abject buyer of whatever is offered. I've been the receiver of such pitches . . . offers of excitement, laughter, suspense, and fame for all who participate in its production . . . and ninety-nine percent of the time, the guy couldn't write a simple scene. Somewhere in *Death of a Salesman* there is undoubtedly a line that covers this personality who can convince without being able to perform. Watch out! Being too loquacious is the danger signal.

Producing in television merely multiplies the occasions on which the foregoing guidelines will be put to use; you have to find many stories and hire many writers. A TV producer must find and woo the writers whose creative instincts coincide with the heartland of his series. Current practice in series production is to give several such writers multiple episode commitments, thus guaranteeing consistency in the product, and often adding up to the number of episodes ordered by the network (leaving little or no room for a free-lance to land a job or get a "spec" script read).

Consistency is important. As I pointed out regarding "The Twilight Zone": tell your appreciative audience the same sort of story, as imaginatively varietal as possible while staying in the same ball park.

Rod and I read and conferred. Out of it all came six writers whose temperament, genes, impulses, and talents meshed with our principles. It was part of my job to keep them coming back to us. They were not on staff, nor could I give multiple commitments, but the welcome mat had a bear trap under it.

And, sure enough, I worked with each one of them differently. In every case, we got acquainted by, first, buying a story of theirs for Rod to adapt, and then asking them:

"What else you got?"

"This. But I want to do the screenplay!"

"Oh?"

Each talent was as distinctive and specialized as I have been describing heretofore. Even their short stories revealed their strengths and their differences.

Richard Matheson was obviously a constructionist; a tight climber from suspense to SUSPENSE; and, as I learned through eight screenplays written by him, all he needed was a springboard—in the case of "The Twilight Zone," a "What if . . .?" He was dependable, sure, and a first draft deliverer.

Two were born storytellers, especially of tall tales, the taller the better. Either Earl Hamner or Monty Pittman could start up yarning in their easy colloquial way, with one listener in the group very late for . . . his wedding, let's say . . . and that groom would wind up listening, anxious for the end to come, even annoyed when it did not come quickly, but unable to break away. Either of these two could sit down in my office, start spinning, and, in twenty minutes, I knew I had a good episode coming once we wrestled the spoken word down to the reality of the filmic word . . .

soaring rhetoric had to go, making sure we had a script that the artists of the set and of post-production could bring to life . . . without losing the imaginative charm of these men's original conception.

Two others were dreamers, in my view. I always had to bring George Johnson and Charles Beaumont down to earth. And their story ideas were always intriguing . . . often adaptations of their previously published short stories . . . and well worth the effort of saying, "Now, let's just take one of those," or, "'The Twilight Zone' only deals with the fifth dimension, not the seventh." Then their craftsmanship took over and a fine screenplay came out—but only after they'd had their fun with Buck.

E. Jack Neuman was my "old China hand," but he was at the time producing two series at once and I couldn't lean on our old friendship for more than one "Twilight Zone" script. Jack knows about everything there is to know about dramatic writing; he's intuitive, a listener, and the trick is: Jack's mechanics never show, only the yarn, the sentiment. Brian Aherne said of "The Trouble With Templeton" episode in which he appeared, "I never read a tougher script that came out so sentimentally moving."

New subject: your conduct with the writer, whether you're headed for a movie theater or a TV screen. The trick is to deal with the writer whom you have selected consistent with your estimate of his peculiar talents. If you picked him because he's a good constructionist, leave him alone on that score. If you know that, no matter what his major strength may be, he is habitually effusive and overlong on dialogue, edit him closely. I take some satisfaction in the fact that of those writers who have said that they liked working with me, half have said it was because I left them alone, and half were laudatory because I dogged their footsteps.

Often, as you work so attentively with a writer, you can guide him to better work . . . better work habits/methods. I recall working with a writer whom I finally saw outside the office . . . at his home for a quiet, two couples dinner; he was a different person (alcohol having nothing to do with it): more articulate, more responsive to others, quicker of mind. I advised him that, as night person, he should do his creative work late in the day, not nine-to-five. He tried it and his output improved in the direction that his night behavior promised—better words, better sentiment, faster. Another writer's work and persona didn't match . . . sober script, spritely person. I told her that her conversation was a lot better than her written dialogue; she should dictate her script work onto a cassette. It worked.

This sort of perception occurs when a producer works for a long time with a writer, sees his character and manner closely, as he must to get the best results, and, in this detachment, observes professionally oriented distinctions that the observed himself does not. Mention them!

But, again, remember, that a producer is not a writer who is too busy to write. But he must recognize good writing and help it along, and recognize poor writing and jump on it. Help the writer with all the awareness of the dramatic process that the pictures and years behind you have taught. As briefly and as pointedly as possible bring up script failures without suggesting solutions unless they are asked for. This is not humility, just reality: he is the better writer. If your criticism or concern or suggestion cannot convince him . . . then go along with the writer and support his way of doing it.

I had two experiences of exactly that kind with Rod Serling.

"Rod! This script! You wrote it too fast and got a little sloppy. The girl doesn't behave the same way twice. You

are ten full pages setting up the situation—y'know the elephant *is* going to disappear."

"Jeez, I hope you're wrong. Call you back in an hour."

An hour later: "You were right. I'll fix it. Lunch?"

Or:

"Rod. I have a feeling that putting this airplane into three different time zones—three different eras—may be pushing credulity pretty hard. Plus that, where in hell do I get the footage of what they see on the ground?"

"I'm coming in this afternoon. We'll talk."

That afternoon:

"Buck, I really think that it's just the way it should be . . . to work. Let's leave it that way."

"Okay."

"And that point-of-view footage? I know you'll work something out." Flattery.

I've seldom lost by going with a good writer's instincts. And I have not kept up a professional relationship with a writer who overcame my reactions and was often wrong.

This cooperation is a game, but it is not adversarial . . . or should not be. Two professionals in a story meeting one of whom is uncle, the producer. Uncle knows that actor Sam Jones cannot deliver long speeches; he starts to get boring. Uncle knows that actress Jane Drew looks lousy in situations where she cannot be extensively made up, so forget the "early in the morning bedroom" scene. However, the writer knows best, even after a producer's misgivings are stated, what really works best for him in the situation he's facing. With any degree of courtesy, these two minds, differently formed, can work to a common goal. But not if the writer automatically sees the producer as an enemy to all good writing . . . or the producer looks upon writers as a necessary evil.

One final matter has to be taken into account. Research. No matter how everyday the script may be, you will profit from having a research service look it over and check out its assumptions: marriage in Kansas can be accomplished on a moments notice—not so, it takes four days between permit and wedding; the speed limit on the German autobahns is 100 km—there is no limit. Etc. The producer should make sure that this research service is available to the various artists who depend a great deal on research for their work to be good: art director, set decorator, prop staff, wardrobe staff, makeup artist, and hairdresser.

Of course, this chapter has been academic if you have bought a perfect screenplay—it's cost effective, it has caught a star, and it is guiltless of any of the dramatic pitfalls we've been going over—long-winded, plot-weak, dull-edged conflicts, etc. You were lucky!

3
THE DIRECTOR

The trick in selecting the best possible director is for the producer to match the peculiarities, the distinctive individualities of the script on his desk, to the skills and tastes of a director.

So, the producer should know the quirks that *this* script presents that promise audience pleasure, and then match them up with the quirks noted on his current director file so as to make the best possible marriage. Is there a dramatic oddity, a milieu outside common experience, or an audience appeal basis (flamboyant action, pratfall farce, sexuality, sentimentality, etc.) that one man will bring through the acting-shooting process better than another?

There are problems other than "picture tone" that color your choice of director.

BUDGET PROBLEMS

This is going to be a tough picture to bring in for the money allotted. And there are directors who are especially skilled at economizing without letting it show (often by rediscovering the principle that small and close is better than big and far) . . . just as there are directors who do not know how to shoot a scene at a football stadium without having the Los Angeles Coliseum at their disposal.

PERFORMANCE PROBLEMS

You have a script that very much depends on fine performances. There are directors who are significantly better than others at leading actors and actresses to their best work. Over and above judging this item of directorial skill, you have to equate the prospective director's way of dealing with performance problems with the performers already tied to the picture: some directors rely almost entirely on the talents that come to the set; "Act!" he says. Well, if your performers are damn good, there's no problem. But if said performers need guidance, they aren't going to get it from this type of director.

Yet other directors have no interest in the training or thought that the player brings with him: he undertakes to show the player every move and nuance of speech; some players need this sort of help, some won't stand for it. And some directors discuss the scene . . . what *he* wants, what the player plans to offer; which is best? There are actors and actresses who respond very affirmatively to this way of going. Seek a match!

Some stars are so painstaking . . . so uncertain of themselves, that it takes a director of great patience to work with them. *Au contraire*, some actors are in such a rush to get done with it that you need a director with a good hammerlock to keep them in front of the camera for Take #2.

COMMAND PROBLEM

Make sure that your choice is a strong minded-person or there will not be the necessary command over the activities of a set full of technicians and players.

(Directorial choices for episodic television are generally far different. In an anthology, like "The Twilight Zone," the standards are much as I have been outlining, but in episodic television, where hewing to the patterns that have made the series successful is the main consideration, the producer tries to build up a team of directors of like disposition and skills so that each episode will seem to be cut from the same piece of movie cloth. You pick them initially for the applicability of their skills to the peculiarities of the series, then hang on to them, not seeking variety.)

Let's take a look at the whole directorial landscape for a moment. There are complications and innuendoes in that craft that are worth understanding minutely, for they have a bearing on how accurately a producer selects the director, then helps him do his very best.

First and foremost and posing the most difficulties is that, unlike the stage director, the screen director weaves the final picture out of bits and pieces made completely out of sequence and/or context. The producer tries his best to see that the shooting schedule is in script order. But that is generally impossible. If you are shooting outdoor locations in Chicago, you shoot all those exterior sequences before coming back to the studio; so the director directs the scene in which the heroine follows her husband out onto the street and pleads for forgiveness long before he stages the immediately preceding scene in which they argue in the living room of their house. At what level of tearfulness does she leave the living room, so as to arrive at that same level in Chicago? Has she thrown the pearl choker at him yet . . . the absence of which reveals the neck scar that proves she is really Jane Smith?

Here's another. How loud and how angrily does the

"heavy" shout into the phone when his first two calls to the hero have yet to be shot elsewhere? It is as if a sculptor first hammered Aphrodite's lips into the mottled block of marble . . . then moved down to her knee . . . then over to her elbow. Will it all come together into an artistic whole? Unfortunately, the dollar considerations of a sensible shooting schedule, of which the producer must always be aware, are constantly forcing the director to join emotional levels here and now to emotional levels that have not yet been shot and thus established.

Then there's the science of placing the camera and moving it about. The camera can convey languor or nervous static; it can look at a scene oddly—tilted or from on high or from ground level; it can distort its vision. (This "camera design" matter is sometimes dealt with by drawing pre-production sketches, called storyboards, that undertakes to nail down every camera set-up in the movie; more about this when I discuss the sketch artist.) The camera's effects are subtle; an audience is seldom conscious of how the camera is carrying them along with the other elements in the film. We'll talk more about this when the cameraman himself is discussed; any director is smart to rely heavily on the cameraman.

Still, the final decision, and responsibility, for the camera's effectiveness is the director's.

Then there are the performers; this is a very complex element in picture making that I'll sort out for you in the appropriate chapter. As I will explain, they are difficult, mostly because they are constantly at career risk. But again, using them, guiding them, helping them meaningfully is the director's major responsibility.

Also, within the director's power to use or leave on automatic pilot is every other element that goes into making a picture . . . be it the props, the wardrobe . . . whatever can help to make the dramatic moment more effective. The director must keep in mind the availability and usefulness of these tools. A love scene, long and wordy to begin with, has a placid, unmoving background; try to help matters by getting the effects man to billow out the window curtains with a false, fan blown wind. The actress playing the part of a frivolous woman is miscast; she ain't frivolous, so get the wardrobe people busy making her *look* frivolous . . . a silly hat, an overdone fur piece.

The director must remember how much the composer can add to a scene. A good love scene rounds out beautifully; then the thoughtful director looks for some extra footage over which the music man can swell the underscore: pan from the loving pair to the window . . . then to the balcony . . . then to the rooftops of Paris in the moonlight.

Or, a performance is not working out . . . the actor doesn't have it. Then the director remembers what the film editor can do: get some footage on other interesting people or aspects of the scene by which the cutter can get away, visually at least, from the bad performance; with just that actor's voice coming over shots of interested listeners, maybe it will play better. A "classic" in this tactic is the close shot of the house cat peeking around the end of the sofa.

With all the mechanisms of movie making at his disposal a director can make an action film more exciting than it was on paper, a farce more hilarious, a love story more heart-rending, a horror-pic more goose-pimply, a too-familiar setting (courtroom, police station, hospital) fresh and interesting again.

How a director uses the artistic skills available to him depends a lot on his temperament . . . how he sees everything, what he sees . . . not solely on how he conceptualizes his movie. I know a director who has an inherent taste for violence; he notices the slightest indication of a violent nature or a violent act . . . the fingers on a hand, writhing for contact with a jaw . . . a stuntman playfully grabbing a fella's head over his shoulder and running that head toward a hanging pot . . . the accidental oil slick around a bear trap. He notices these things in his daily life and on the set; and that director is damn good at violent action pictures.

However, I know another director whose inclination is to turn his head away from the bloody brutality of a cat overtaking a mouse, jaws open; that director won't see nor imagine the violent actions that will make a violence-oriented picture better. On the other hand, this same director can direct soft material and never let it get sloppy, saccharine; he sees the soft gesture . . . the little token of affection . . . on the set or in daily life. Both these men, the harsh and the gentle, have stored up devices within themselves to portray what your screenplay, whichever way it tends, better.

So, directors are artists, and as such, are the result of their persona, shaped by their life experiences.

Have you noticed . . . it's interesting . . . that both the producer and the director achieve their creative visions by motivating others; both could do their job without hands, for they touch nothing.

Time and again, "The Twilight Zone" scripts handed me tough problems in director selection. Which director could best deal with a really fine script that called for avoiding the sight of any of the performers' faces until the last two minutes of the twenty-six? Here's a swell story about five characters whose entire screen time is spent in some inexplicable place that proves in the end to be the bottom of a huge barrel. This story starts with a locale entitled: INTERIOR LIMBO. Then there's this interesting fella who talks for twenty-two minutes with an equally interesting fella . . . his alter ego, same actor. This one has to be done in the style of the old Mack Sennett two-reelers. Some were dollar problems: An asteroid landscape? A nuclear blast . . . a wrecked, weed-grown town . . . ?

Now, there's not a director worth his Guild card who wouldn't tackle any one of those problems, but, like so many of the producer's choices, there is one pick which is the best of all, if only by a few percentage points. I didn't bat a thousand, but there were several selections, even many, that were made better by a consideration being given to a potential director's personal tastes, quirks, inclinations, habits.

I will leave this discussion of director selection with one hard-to-attain requirement: a good director should improve the material he is handed, not merely get it up there on the screen where you can see it and hear it. In bringing the script to the screen, he should boost its emotional impact by several notches . . . make it funnier, grab you tighter by the throat; whatever its dramatic objectives, they should be stronger on the screen than they were on the printed page. A tone should have been set that was not possible for the writer to establish . . . a style in harmony with the subject that, again, could not be put to paper. About the only way you can check out a director for this capacity to improve what he is given by way of a script is to read a script which he has directed, then see the finished picture.

Finally, there are ways to investigate the talents of the director you are inclined to hire. Talk to the assistant director on one of his pictures about how it goes on the set; talk to the editor on one of his pictures about how his shooting plan came together in the cutting room. Those are the two areas of expertise about which you are most interested and, lacking a crystal ball, know the least about when going in with an unfamiliar director; his talents with story and casting you will learn in time to shore up his deficiencies, but conduct on the set (where there is no time for shoring up) and how that segmented film comes together after the shooting expense should be known up front.

Let us turn now to how you, as producer, conduct yourself with this artist whom you have chosen for his emotional and technical fit to the material.

First off, you meet together in order to deal with any objections the director may have to the script. Listen carefully, for, if you have chosen well, there's a new, fresh talent aboard who could very well have ideas that improve the dialogue or the plotting. I advise bringing the writer back in to get *that* reaction to the director's suggestions; then you'll argue (or agree), but, bottom line, I am usually against major changes unless the writer and I both conclude that the director's notions are an improvement.

And this brings up the whole question of script changes that come after the producer, director, writer (perhaps the star) have come to agreement . . . be they now, during preparation, or later, during shooting. I tend to be very reluctant about late changes in dialogue or structure because they tend to be last-minute ones; the script has been too patiently crafted for tardy, hasty ideas to be an improvement; in fact, they may do harm. Character growth and plot development has been structured into the script, point by point; an ill-thought out change or deletion can drop out an important element in that overall plan. Be careful!

After script matters are settled, you start discussions with the other creative artists—casting director, production designer, cameraman, set decorator, wardrobe designer, makeup and hairdress artists—to square away everyone's intentions. Here too there may be heated arguments between qualified artistic professionals that the producer must adjudicate. I'll take up the nature of these discussions in the appropriate chapter.

So the producer and the director conspire before shooting starts just like the coach and the quarterback before the game . . . the trainer and the jockey before the race . . . the driver of the get-away car and the gunman before the hold-up. Talk out the problems, agree on their solutions, effect the solutions to the furthest point you can short of their use on the set . . . *then, Producer, step back and let the director alone.* For out there on the field, or on the far turn, or in the bank vault . . . matters are proceeding at a cruelly fast and expensive clip. Do not interrupt the quick flow of tense creative work . . . of quick and compatible adaptations from the master plan . . . that a shooting set demands. However, if the director starts to vary unreasonably or widely from the preproduction plans (or blatantly ignore them, or fail to deliver), then the producer must step in and call a recess— be it for ten minutes or a day—and demand adjustment, or, on occasion, the director's departure.

Nothing can water down the alcohol level of a motion picture more certainly than for the set to be run by committee. Or by "I wouldn't have done it that way," remarks; for, come to find out, the reason that the director didn't care whether Jane smiled or not in this shot is that she smiled in the closeup yesterday . . . which is the shot that will certainly be used in the cut picture.

(Sure, I know that some fine football coaches send in every play from the bench. So did David O. Selznick; he memoed every move on the set. A friend of mine, dialogue director on *Gone With the Wind,* got a Selznick memo reading: "Be sure that you don't teach southern accents to the actors playing Union officers and soldiers." But I don't recommend this practice to you; it runs too close to the danger of the "too many cooks" aphorism proving true.)

Indeed, the producer should not be needed on the set except as a parental figure who drops in from time to time to reassure the crew, and especially the director, that outside matters, lying ahead and beyond the scope of the microcosm that they're working on, are being taken care of. As I have remarked before, the producer's main job is to see that that shooting process be so well planned that it proceeds smoothly and productively, day by day, without ill-considered, on-the-spot, snap judgments.

As with the writer, if you have chosen your director well, let him prevail when you come to an argumentative tie during the preparation period. Make sure that he realizes that he risks losing a smidgen or two of autonomy at the next turn of the road if he is wrong. If he is smart, he knows that he works best when his judgment is widely trusted, and he will not risk that atmosphere of approval unless he is sure he's right. On the other hand, the producer cannot afford to give the director a completely free hand—there are money limitations, there are commitments to others that were made before the director came on the job (like: no risks will be taken with the rating system; no script changes by others than the original writer; no cheating on the child labor laws; etc.).

Then there's the old saying that "nothing destroys a talent like giving him/her everything he/she wants." An imaginative director can easily levitate himself right into an inventory of storytelling elements that hurt his picture: too much grandeur, too many spices.

Indeed, golden riches can often come for all hands by pinching pennies. When an expensive scene or series of scenes must be done, the producer should challenge the director and the other artists involved in that expense to sweat over it a bit; try to convey the same impact with less material. To reduce that theory to a true story . . . I had the pleasure of working on a picture with Jean Renoir, closely enough to comfortably ask a personal question: "How come so many fine foreign directors do less well in the U.S.?" He told me a story to illustrate his theory that European production, often being a hand-to-mouth money process, gives rise to stresses that in turn incite invention; whereas here, where money is plentiful, there is often a lack of creative challenge, which tends to stifle filmic ingenuity. On a sequence that he was to shoot in the Gare du Nord the next day with 100 extras and two trains, Jean was told the night before that it could not be afforded . . . no money for any of it! Jean was dismayed. The next morning, heart in mouth, he asked his production manager for a steam engine's drivewheel, some steam, one extra, and a railroad ticket; he then conveyed the story information necessary with those three props (and was widely praised, especially in the critical press, for that artful little sequence). On the other hand, on his first picture in this country, he dropped into a big New Orleans hotel on his way west because the story he was to tell took place in a big hotel. It was exemplary—a courtyard surrounded by three stories of balconied rooms. He told his producer and the studio head about this hotel and how well it fitted their needs. Then, three weeks into the picture's preparation as to cast, wardrobe, etc., Jean was invited to visit Stage 13; there was almost exactly what he had seen in New Orleans! No need to stretch the mind . . . no need to be filmic about that hotel . . . shooting here was purely reportorial. The producer hadn't pinched the penny.

There are circumstances when the producer will want to act in exactly the opposite fashion: instead of tightening the rein in order to inspire ingenuity, he may urge the director to dream the impossible dream—stretch your mind and that of other creators on hand to achieve a highly desirable, heretofore unfamiliar, effect; maybe we can afford it! Due to the unusual demands in some of Rod Serling's scripts, I often said to directors, "Come on. That's the easy way . . . the too-often-done way . . . to see a man talking to himself." Or "Let's do better than just have the little girl disappear in a double exposure dissolve." Directors are so surprised when a producer suggests the pursuit of an idea that may cost an extra buck that they really put on their thinking caps.

Of course, be easily available to the director during the shooting period; close as he is to today's work, he is depending on the producer to maintain an overview. Often he needs someone to talk to about his problems, but let him bring it up. He has a skilled professional in every applicable craft at his fingertips, so his chats with the producer will probably be general and overall. These little talks generally occur after you and the director have seen dailies together; the situation is a little like sharing a meal together, the director being the host: you are approving, letting him bring up the obvious flaws in the work . . . then you discuss how to deal with those flaws (re-takes, re-casting, etc.); then, in the same spirit that you would find something wrong with the salad course, talk about how the lighting seems a little dark, or that actress is rather more bawdy in her behavior than you thought had been agreed upon, etc. The point being: get your reaction into the directorial process gently; a good director will listen to and profit from suggestions, but he will find that DE-MANDS are disruptive of that flow of intensive creative work that I have described before as the director's lot.

And you'll have to be patient about the director's complaints . . . about one of the crew who is misbehaving, a player stinks, the tightness of the schedule; you fix these matters if you can, because keeping that directorial mind focused on the storytelling machinery, not low-level squabbles, serves you best. Get the prop man in line; keep visitors off the set if they annoy; ask the studio head not to comment on the dailies . . . whatever helps keep that director's mind on his proper business.

But after the shooting is over, another code of conduct comes into play. The time pressures are over; whatever is done now is not being set in concrete. (The post production process is discussed more fully later in this book when editing, dubbing, and scoring are covered). On most features, the director will take a very meaningful hand in these labors.

A note here about the director in television: they work only in the limelight of a few hot days of preparation and the shoot itself. Thus, it is a producer's medium, by and large, because the producer is the only creative force who is always on hand to oversee series consistency. In the first year of "The Twilight Zone," there were at least twenty different directors, spread every which way at other work while story preparation, scripting, and, later, post-production chores were going on. The producer, at any given moment, is working with writers on several shows (working per the feature film guidelines covered in Chapter Two), preparing at least one for shooting with director A, watching director B on the shooting stage (these last two chores according to the feature film precepts in the current Chapter), and is working with three sets of editors, one composer, and the dubbing crew (working per the standards of performance which I will cover in later chapters). Of all those chores, the director is only available for the preparation and the shoot. Director A is shooting when his last picture is being dubbed; he just cannot have a voice in two places . . . so the producer does it. And the producer must earn the confidence of good directors in his post-production skills, or they won't be coming back to work the show.

In this post-production time, other professionals take over the film's destiny, and the footage in hand is their raw material; the director (in the time-luxury of the feature picture field) joins the producer in a strong managerial capacity, giving way nonetheless to superior artisans even if a grinding of teeth is necessary. If the director wants to spend the time (and most of them do), he is contractually entitled to command the second cut; the editor will have been assembling film as the shooting went along, and be ready to show a first "rough cut" a week or two after the closedown to the producer and the director. Then the director re-cuts to *his* taste and shows it to the producer; whereupon the arguing starts. (Unless the director, being powerful, has the right of "final cut.") Again, as in pre-production, this work in completing the picture is a shared responsibility between the director and the producer and the post-production specialists (sometimes the studio management gets in the act; then it's just power politics that determines the final release version).

Again, I tend to have my own views fall into second place nest to the "pro" in his area. I will insist that my ideas be tried (the director's too, of course), but, in the muck and mire of a stand-off on a point, give way to the post production specialist.

Throughout all this, there is one very sticky wicket for the producer . . . when he must call the shots in a disagreement between the director and other creative people. This can begin as a disagreement between the writer and the director: the director wants changes in the script. Often, his "director's eye" for a setting or his "ear" for a sound will improve matters to everyone's satisfaction; but sometimes there is complete disagreement. Then the producer has to make a ruling and hope for the best; usually it works well to settle on the side of the script; it's been thought about, considered, and mulled for a long time.

Rehearsal time is valuable, economically and artistically. Not only are differences of opinion often settled, but strength is lent to the path that the script and the directors and the actors are planning to be on. On "The Twilight Zone" we saved money by rehearsing for one day (a "down" day for a reasonably expensive crew—most management hates to hear of a full crew that isn't busily exposing film) preparatory to three days shooting. Thus, there were no costly surprises during shooting (the cameraman moans, "I didn't know you were going to play that scene in front of the fireplace); each line was heard aloud and, the writer generally being there, corrections were made as necessary; and, most important, when we had to shoot about eight to ten pages a day (as you do today), it was good that the performers had their lines in their heads and their characterizations thought out.

A word of caution about rehearsals: don't let them run on too long; movie trained performers can get stale. They are not like stage actors, getting better and deeper into a part each day; they are used to giving their best very near the word "go."

For the director, rehearsals are a great benefit since he gets to experiment with the readings, the words, the camera moves, etc.

There are some aides to the director that the producer should think about. Some pictures support a Dialogue Director, especially if the director wants one. The main function here is to rehearse the actors in their lines. Because movies are shot so out of sequence, it is pointless for an actor to "know" his part . . . some scenes won't come up for weeks. So it's a day-by-day learning process; for some, learning the day's dialogue is a wearing labor, some will easily have all of today's work down cold . . . and not remember a word of yesterday's work. The dialogue director who is on the ball will search out the actors when they have a moment free, be they in makeup, or snoozing outside the stage door, waiting for their scene to come up, and offer to run the lines with them; sometimes two players, having a scene together, will want to go over it together. All this is very helpful providing the dialogue director does not take on directorial functions; just the words, thank you.

Two other major helpers to the director, when circumstances call for them, are a Dance Director and/or a Second Unit Director. The first is a dance designer who, in cooperation with Director, Producer, Cameraman and the Music Coordinator, masterminds a dance sequence that fits the script; if it is a musical movie, there will be several dance numbers . . . elaborate and leaving reality behind. These musical numbers are often so much a highlight of the film that they are virtually a directorial assignment quite apart from the storytelling/dialogue portions. Then, as producer, you have two operations to oversee, and see to it that they inter-lock with dramatic interest. I will have more to say about this phase of the producer's responsibility in my chapter on music.

Some directors can command, on account of their experience in the field or on account of sheer negotiating power, almost total say-so over the musical numbers . . . overseeing the dance director's rehearsals, ordering changes, etc. It is then the producer's responsibility to judge whether or not the director is improving on the dance director's work or not. You are often back to the credo I've offered up before, "Go with the most pro," if the director's improvements are not self-evident.

It is wise to bring in a good dance director when you have a dance hall situation, be it period at Versailles or tonight at the Madhouse. Give him a day or two rehearsal with the dancing extras so that it will go promptly and handsomely on the set.

The Second Unit Director becomes a necessity when there are big action sequences in which the principals are not involved (or are doubled with stunt people). Here we are getting into a matter of production planning and budgeting that I will take up when I get into the production staff and its work. Suffice it to say, for now, that the principal director is very much involved in the second unit plans, for their execution must fit in exactly with his work on the stage, especially in that close camera work on the performers who have been doubled in the second unit footage. The producer can only rest well here when he knows that everyone is aware of what the other guy is doing.

There is one special circumstance in which the producer adopts a different work pattern than any other: when the director is also the writer. For my money, the writer-director hyphenation is ideal. He imagined it as he wrote, now he goes about putting his mental pictures onto film. Who better? Just help him; come to understand, from the script and your pre-production meetings, what he wants to fulfill his plan and see to it that he gets it.

There is yet another circumstance calling for yet another tactic: sometimes you find yourself working with an actor-director. This too is a very natural and productive hyphen-ation; he has been on the receiving end of efforts from entire crews . . . wardrobe people, cameramen, you name 'em. Therefore he is at ease with the same professionals in the director's role; and he's about certain to be good with the performers. (If you have decided that performances are a key to your picture working, it might be worthwhile to look around for a good actor who likes, and comprehends, the script on your terms.) The producer's role is the same in every way except that he must act in the director's role occasionally . . . be on the set to help judge how the shot worked; the director is often acting in the shot and needs an okay. It may be that the actor/director will want someone else to be his "checker" . . . the cameraman or the dialogue director . . . in which case you have to watch matters for a few days to make sure that appointee is good enough; if he is, let it go; if not, take over or find a new procedure.

Here is as good a place as any to indict the Producer-Director, the one-man show practice. To begin with, when the director is directing, the producer is out to lunch—that job is not being done, or is being undertaken by an underling without either authority or experience at the command level. But the main loss to picture quality in total creative autonomy being placed in one person is that the holder of it is never challenged in his decisions. And, as I've noted elsewhere, it is healthy and rewarding for all motion picture participants to be contested in their plans when difficult twists and turns show up. I don't care how preeminent a director (or writer, or gaffer, or prop man) may be, he is put higher onto his toes when someone else poses another way of accomplishing something. As I've also said a few pages ago, the expert should prevail, but being compelled to think twice or three times about a move almost ensures that the move is the correct one . . . or that a better move has surfaced out of the discussion.

I save the toughest to swallow and the worst until last: you are hired for the Producer role on a picture on which the Director has been given total autonomy . . . a bargained-for position often demanded by the powerful. In this delicate position, you must be as benign and helpful an assistant as possible; your job is to see to it that this man's vision is realized. The trick is to make an agreement early with that director: you are not a spy for the front office, and there is profit in listening to your counsel. Agree in the usual, day-to-day meetings, on what must be done to succeed with this picture (his opinion prevailing) and you promise, and that promise is accepted, that you will adhere to these plans as you do your off-stage, days-ahead-of-shooting work. If this director is distrustful, autocratic, or an artistically unguided missile, the producer has his hands full: he can quit, report the impasse to management, or lay in a supply of sedatives and battle it out.

4
THE CAST

Performers come in all sizes and shapes and degrees of talent . . . *and* degrees of appropriateness to the part that they are called upon to play. There is, however, a safe generalization to guide the producer in a general way as he goes into the maze of choices: there are two basic types— performers and personalities. The former, to some logical degree can play a wide, wide range of roles, portraying people completely unlike themselves . . . basing their performance on observation and an intellectualization of what that character *must* be like. The latter, the personality, probably has succeeded in the profession just as he is— charming, funny by nature, easily handsome or beautiful, naturally menacing even while eating breakfast; this one is not dumb nor unwilling to think out variations on his own persona . . . he's never had to. It takes training . . . schooling . . . to behave differently than you *are*. Again, a generalization: most stars are personalities, and most supporting players, however big a name, are performers.

However hard you work at casting, it is still a guessing game.

The producer is concerned with three phases of casting—

three different kinds. The first is star casting, the second is the casting of the featured players, and the third is the casting of the small, one-day bits. They all take a different approach.

In star casting you are setting the financial and quality tone of your picture according to the propriety and popularity of the star or stars you induce to play the parts. Their price dictates your budget. For instance, you cast Tom Cruise in a picture; at his price, which currently can be between $10 million and $15 million, everything else in the picture seems to rise . . . the shooting time, the cost of the director, the cost of the various subsidiary privileges that go with a picture that starts with a high cost mandate. If you cast a lesser player, maybe even as good an actor but without the wide popular appeal nor the high price, everything scales down; the length of shooting time, the cost of the director, the entire attitude toward the picture is tighter-fisted because its potential market is less. Whereas the potential market for the Tom Cruise picture is almost limitless. Sometimes you *have* to go after a star of that magnitude because the basic and irreducible costs of making that particular picture are so high on account of, let's say, special effects or stunt scenes or whatever, that only a star of demonstrable drawing power can justify the risks of that budget. Then there are stories that do not have an inherently high cost; you have a choice between going for a big star and upping your basic budget by somewhat more than his price . . . or you can go for a lesser player and stay very moderate. The consideration here is how much will that picture bring in in the marketplace. And that is anybody's guess.

We should not forget the opportunity to make a picture without any stars whatever—good actors to be sure—but depending for box office entirely on the appeal of the subject matter, be it a fright movie or a version of Ibsen. Think back to *Sex, Lies and Videotape*; they weren't stars then.

The perils of this choice between lavish and tight . . . big stars, big budget . . . or good actors, small budget . . . becomes a little more apparent if you think back to *Rain Man* with Dustin Hoffman and Tom Cruise. Top stars at top cost and made extravagantly. It was very, very successful. It could have been made very inexpensively with no names whatsoever, merely good actors, for the production dollar demands were light. The producers obviously made a very good decision in this case because they grossed and netted considerably more at this expense than they would have enjoyed at a lesser expense—and its probable consequence: a far lower box office.

However, there's another side to that coin. In a fairly recent picture, the producers combined three major, costly stars in a picture of modest budget requirements having to do with a small family's household wars. It was very thoughtfully, very carefully done and somehow did not catch on, and, either money could have been saved or, conceivably, one could have made a little, if it had been made with a far more modest cast and at a far more modest cost.

In short, it's a gamble, with all the elements that go into gambling, when the producer chooses between a high-cost cast and a low-cost cast. (Of course, that is providing he has the option of going to a low-cost budget with that particular script . . . its production demands being inherently expensive, no matter who is in it.) It is the current thinking among the studios that, when it is possible to attach big stars to a script, it is better to go that high-cost route than it is to go with a more modest picture. For some reason in the current market, an expensively made, luxurious-looking picture with big stars warrants the added investment on a dollar-for-dollar, bank-thinking basis as compared to going with a very modest picture and fighting the battle of getting theater time for a no-name picture which will probably draw modest crowds. It is an easily demonstrable truth that a big box-office name or two will get distributor and theater owner enthusiasm . . . and then great audiences for at least a short time . . . the short time it takes for them to smell out whether it is a picture they like or not. If it sails, everyone is delighted that there was a star name to get them into the theater, spread the word, and guarantee a long, profitable run for all; if it plays to smaller and smaller audiences as the days go by, despite the stars, the gamble-bait has failed.

Having decided that the economics or the aesthetics of your script deserves (demands . . . could use nicely) a star, or even a lesser light, a "name" player, you thus embark on either a game of money raising, or of power politics, or of self-promotion, or of all three; it's according to where you stand in the business community. If you're a friend of the player, you get a "read" and, if affirmative, a reaction that you can use to get on with the production procedures. Failing that bit of luck, you need an important chunk of money to tie down either a name player or a star, for agents are very watchful of their client's scheduling and of their marketability. They don't want to block out next October and November for their star's appearance in your picture and then find out that the money isn't there and the picture is off: no money and an angry, idle client. Nor do they want you to be able to "shop" their client's name and affirmative reaction around town, using the power of the name to put together a deal. *A valid money guarantee up front, or no dice.* For a big star, the agent will want a pay-or-play commitment with a start date (even from a major studio) . . . the pay starts then, whether the picture does or not. For even a name player, an agent will also want a pay-or-play commitment with a start date from a reputable independent or a major studio (unless the name player sees a great opportunity for career advancement in your script and is willing to

bend a lot to get the part). But from a small independent
whose finances are not known to him, the agent might well
ask that his client, be he star or "name," see his going price
up front in cash with a firm play date *before* he and his client
will even read the script; then, if they like it, that up-front
money will be kept by them whether the picture goes or
not.

So, if you have a working arrangement with a financially
solid independent or a major studio, you submit your script
to the star through his agent with their financial backing and
approval (they probably know the project well, having
backed you in its development).

If you are without meaningful ties to money, you hit the
streets, seeking the enthusiasm of a solid independent or a
studio, or, if you are ingenious in such matters, raise money
from investors, from junk bond merchants, or from an
investment consortium of dentists from Toledo. (I know of a
picture that sailed with the latter.)

When you go after a big star, the cat quite often has a
long tail. The agent's packaging instinct will come into play
immediately; he will begin to think of which other client he
can attach to the project as a subsidiary or side price for
pressing on with this deal. His client director. Or perhaps
the leading woman role.

On the other hand, I must say, before I lose every agent/
friend I have, that with a good script in hand you can go to
one of the four or five big agencies and say, "Here's a fine
script. Flesh it out from your client list and we'll take it to
Fox. Huh?" If they see how to put flesh on those bones,
they'll do it and do it well.

To add to the complications, the star himself may insist
on a relatively short list of directors from which the producer
must choose in order to get that star's services; this seems
perfectly normal to me since most stars have a talent and
reputation and an earning capacity to protect. And it cer-

tainly would not be wise of them to go out into the risk territory of a picture without knowing that the guidance on the set, and, indeed, sometimes the guidance back at your office, is of first rate order and fine reputation.

These negotiations are usually one trade-off after another: a four-week variable in the start date if you use this director; ten working weeks for the fee instead of eight if you cast this actress; etc., etc.

It is quite surprising to find that almost any actor or actress who's name you or I would recognize takes the demanding position regarding money that I have outlined above when it comes to a submission from someone other than a studio. Names that you have to scratch your head to recall will ask for a full fee in good faith before they will read. This again is in protection of their wish not to be shopped around town; you must not be surprised by its occurrence.

Now you turn your attention to the casting of feature players (and by that I mean strong parts that are in subsidiary roles) and to the casting of bit parts which again may be very important, but are only on for a short time and cost relatively little compared to major stars. To make this job easy on the producer, there is a casting director assigned to almost any picture. These people are quite remarkable in the encyclopedic knowledge they have of the actors in Los Angeles, in New York, in London, in the theater, on the variety stage, all over the place. I think that they must constantly spend their evenings at some sort of theater. And their knowledge is not merely an acquaintance with names so that they come to your desk with a long list that they've culled from the actors directory. The best casting directors bring you their choice, their opinion of what is going to be the best possible casting for this featured role or this bit role. (Be wary of the casting director who brings you great long lists of the right age and sex; those are easy to compile and show no thought given to performance values.)

Incidentally, a good casting director's perspicacity about playing values may lead to an off-beat choice that enhances your film; so-and-so is known for tough-guy roles, but, unknown to most, is his capacity to play soft and sentimental; he is not just a well projected personality. A coup!

Besides being aware of various performers' talents the casting director is also well informed as to their going prices. You must make him aware of your budget so that he does not tease you with the prospect of casting people whom you cannot afford.

One common way to pinpoint a player's suitability for the role is to have him "read" for the part; i.e. sit in the producer's office and read the role from a script copy (having been given it overnight for home study or for only fifteen or twenty minutes in the outer office). One does this especially when the part seems to be somewhat different from the player's obvious personality; with a little experience almost anyone can play himself, but it takes special skills of a really high level of artistry to portray someone outside one's own personality and range of experience. Incidentally, the performer is in no way helped in this reading by the fact that the "actor" with whom he is reacting, and who is feeding him his lines, is probably the producer or the casting director.

At such a reading the director can learn a lot about the performer's talents by asking for a different interpretation of the lines . . . a different cadence . . . sadder . . . lighter; the performer's ability to change gears quickly and accurately bodes well for the results in front of the camera. Producer! Insist on readings (or a view of a scene or two from a picture with a similar role), for there is nothing so stomach dropping as discovering, on the set, that this player will not do.

In the case of a difference of opinion about a player and his suitability for a given role I would go with a good casting director's opinion almost every time—unless the director, who rightly has a strong hand in this process, has worked with that actor. Then I think probably the director's voice should prevail.

Every producer has an anecdote or two to tell about casting. During the making of "The Twilight Zone" it's not fair to say that Rod and I were in the business of casting stars. But quite often we reached for people who did not work in the television field. Rod could even have had that personality in his mind as he wrote. It was our experience that the agent clamly would say, "Gee, Buck, she doesn't do television." And I'd say, "Well, have her read this script." And then in a few days I would get a call back saying "Well, she still doesn't do television, but she'll do this." This of course is a comment on Rod Serling's writing and the adventuresomeness that quite often went with our plots— they provided the sort of acting opportunity that most performers relish. Quite often, a player who was very protective of his reputation and concerned that his talents always be used properly would come into our office on a tentative basis because he was not quite sure whether these folks down at "The Twilight Zone" had their heads screwed on right or not. Agnes Moorehead came into my office to meet director Doug Heyes with a most suspicious cast to her features . . . she having read a fifteen-page script with no dialogue. It took Heyes a better part of an hour to help her come to understand how that picture was going to be made in such a way that she would be delighted to perform it. Point: sometimes the script quality will carry the day better than money.

Again referring to "The Twilight Zone" experience, stars

often need to be comfortable about the quality of production that they are about to submit their reputation to. Early in the first season of production, before the series had hit the air and established a standard for good material, good performances, and high-quality production values, I quite often had difficulty with people who had very substantial names in motion pictures of that time. Dan Duryea, Ida Lupino, Gig Young, Ed Wynn, Burgess Meredith, Richard Conte, all needed convincing that we were up to doing as good a picture as the script was good. They were saying, "This is a hell of a script, but can you deliver equal performance so far as crew and director are concerned . . . especially on that short TV shooting schedule?" All I could do in those cases was put my eyes to heaven and say, "We'll do our very best." And it always turned out that by the end of the first day's work, the general competence of the crew and the seriousness with which everybody was going about their work convinced them and they were completely comfortable and happy for the remainder of the shooting period. I never received a cast regret.

In feature production, too, the producer can expect to be closely inspected by any star he may be after . . . unless his reputation is very solid. The player will want to be sure that he is in good hands; might even want to know who the co-players will be. And the reputation of the director will be very important; it's happened more than once that a star has been eager to play a role and, yet, will haggle to the point of dropping out if the director is not to his liking. Once again, it is guarding that hardly-won stardom.

Now we can turn to a new subject with regard to cast, and that is the producer's responsibility for helping to keep that cast productive and happy and in good form. The assistant director is a great aid to the producer in this matter because, being on the set and having the equanimity of that set very much on his mind, he can get to the producer and tell him of things that are going amiss that would be time-wasting for the director to straighten out (the director has the day-to-day problem of getting the best from those performers and maintaining a calm relationship with them that does not admit of any extraneous problems befogging a good performance). These problems can run all the way from too many martinis at lunch, to dissatisfaction with the dressing room, to ego competition with the other players. (I can remember when I was at RKO in an associate producer role that there was an actor who was quick and alert in the morning, and sluggish in the afternoon: ten seconds between line cues. It became my role to make up a friendship with that player to the point where he and I lunched together . . . in the commissary where there was no bar.)

Especially among big stars there are ego problems in terms of precedence and shall we say "pecking order." There's a famous story that comes out of Warner Brothers about two star actresses who were on the same picture. And neither one would suffer a call to the set that had her standing around for ten seconds waiting for the other. So it was the assistant director's problem to make sure that their summonses to the set were so neatly timed that they arrived simultaneously. This ego problem can also have to do with the size of dressing rooms and the size of the trailer on location and the choice of hair dresser, etc. The producer must not be surprised when very odd ego problems arise with the performers.

You mustn't mistake my telling of these foibles on the part of stars and even smaller actors as a disrespectful joke at their expense. Their reputations and their incomes and their faces are on the firing line on the set. It is either funny or it isn't. It's either melodramatic or it isn't. It's either a lovely love story or it is not a lovely love story. The lights are right or they're not right. The director's decision that that take is perfect is, God willing, a correct decision. But the performers are the ones whose faces and talents are exposed, in full light, for the world to look at and, God forbid, decide that they did badly. Which means that they won't get paid as much for their next picture or they won't be wanted for the script that's coming along that they'd like to play. They have a lot at stake with every day's work. And quite often and quite humanly they decide to make a fuss on one score when they are disturbed on a completely different score. Many is the time when I've been aware of a fuss on the set having to do with a dressing room that was too small or a makeup man was being objectionable, and come to find out it was nothing more than the fact that the player was in a small panic about the scene coming up and wanted to postpone it until he had gotten his mind clearly wrapped around doing that scene without revealing to all that he wasn't up to the job. This sort of difficulty partly arises from the fact that their work is done at other people's direction . . . Right now! "Camera! Action!" A writer could not write on a stop-and-go basis. A businessman could not make sound decisions on the basis of somebody else saying "Action." A painter could not undertake a portrait on the basis of a sitter coming in and sitting down and saying "Go." Handling the performers with delicacy is a task for both the director and the producer. But it should not be looked upon as an unusual or unwelcome task.

In the two aspects of television there is a different chore for the producer. In series television, quite often the series itself creates the star. It is considered relatively safe to initiate a series with a actor who is appropriate but is not widely known. And, more often than not, in series television, the other roles, which are sometimes featured and sometimes are almost starring, are also filled with people whose names are not widely known but whose reputations are sound. Because series television is very, very hard on the actor, the producer is wise who picks experienced people if he is going to make his series pictures on budget, on time and with a consistent level of performance.

However, it often happens that as a series goes into its third and fourth year and is an acclaimed success, and is probably good for another two or three years, the star has a tendency to take over the management of the series; he views himself, and his agent also views him, as pivotal to the series continuing. Everybody else could die or quit and the series would still go on. If he decides to go elsewhere, or find that his demands are not being met, the series stops. This is enough to make a producer gnash his teeth but, yet, it is unfortunately quite understandable because the television series star probably has his creative life at stake in the series. Very seldom does a television star finish a series and then go on to another or to motion picture fame. There are very few whom I can think of with their feet solidly planted in both aspects of motion-picture making. Therefore that television star feels that his sensitivity to the way that series works is very, very important and that his creative and, conceivably, his monetary life is at stake. He would be the last to say that the producer had been making bad decisions for those two or three years of success but he feels that by now he knows more about that character and that series, having played it day after day after day, and knows it in a more visceral way than any producer could. And, therefore, in those late days when you are fighting to remain interesting with the same characterization and the same sort of dramatic problems, he feels that he is better suited to picking the course that the series must take to stay fresh. Naturally, in my opinion he is wrong because he casts himself there in the role of both judge and jury and will tend to make mistakes by not having any opposition to overcome. Overcoming opposition is often the test of a good idea. And the lack of opposition to overcome quite often brings bad ideas, untouched and unremarked upon, right out into the open for everyone to criticize. But this fact of life in series television, while not always true by any means, is nevertheless a perfectly human reaction to events.

In motion pictures for television there is yet another attitude to take. These two-hour to six-hour specials most often need a name of some kind to attract the audience, unless the subject matter is indeed the star. If the network lets the public know that tonight's special is based on the famous murders in St. Petersburg, Florida, last year, perhaps a star is not necessary. But, in most motion pictures for television, the subject matter is not necessarily the leading attraction. Therefore, you need a name of some kind and most often that name is drawn from television itself. Very seldom does a motion picture name of any kind appear in movies-of-the-week. I do not believe that this is snobbishness, I think it goes back to my former mention of a star's concern for his standing as a performer: his status will be put in jeopardy while speeding along, doing a two-hour picture in three weeks. And it could very well be argued that for the television audience, television stars mean more to them than motion picture stars.

But, be they motion picture stars or television stars, the producer has the same obligation to handle those players in a way that indicates his understanding of the difficulties of their task. The television players deserve even more consideration because they're being asked to perform at a far faster pace. A feature will very well shoot at the rate of three or four pages a day and feel it is doing very well. Whereas a television motion picture may have to shoot as fast as eight, nine, ten pages a day. As a consequence there are fewer set ups on a given scene and, therefore, fewer times for the actor to get into the part. More than ever his performance is a fish-or-cut-bait challenge. A "Do it now; do it your best because you don't get to do it over again" sort of situation.

And if I have made any point clear at all in these remarks up to now, it is that the producer has to be sensitive to the human condition, to the human feeling about things . . . because you are in a sensory art. You are working in an art form depending on human feeling and on human reactions. You should not be surprised by, indeed be prepared to deal with, human reactions that are off the wall, mind boggling and even aggressive. It's human nature, and whistling the song of human nature in all its aspects and meanings is the business you're in.

5
THE EXTRAS

Many a picture will go by without the producer having had to pay any attention to this phase of the production. Central Casting provides extra casting services for most of the studios and many of the independents; it is a sound organization to whom the assistant director addresses his needs, and they take up their phones and fill the bill.

The only occasion for the producer to get to work on the extras is in case they are slightly off, let's say, in age or in wardrobe. It often happens that in the hurly-burly of filling an overnight extra order (that may have been less descriptive than it should have been) Central Casting or one of the several casting facilities available will send people to fill a high school auditorium who are not quite teenagers. Or send people to an informal country-club dance in full dress. Then the director, assistant director, and producer have to ad lib some solution: get the high school group into their shirt sleeves and plan to keep the camera at a distance; send 'em home for a change in wardrobe, in which case the director has to ad lib for a while, waiting; shoot, perhaps, closeups out of sequence, while waiting; bring in a flat and get those closeup retakes of the leading lady that have been dangling in the schedule for a week, etc. (Incidentally, any extra wardrobe that is logically within the scope of anybody's closet can be requested by the assistant director.)

The absence of a Central Casting type service, either by choice or for economy, or because you are on a distant location, is usually solved by a location manager assistant who spends his time recruiting in likely places to fill the need: the state unemployment offices, the local high school, the local Elks club, etc.

A great many states have a Film Commissioner whose job it is to induce motion picture companies to come and film in that state. And quite often he will have made arrangements prior to your arrival for someone to have recruited extras.

This area is the least of your concerns.

6
THE PRODUCTION STAFF

Herein are the producer's front-line troops in terms of managing the day-to-day production process. While preparing to shoot, and during shooting itself, this group of five (sometimes more if the load is heavy) are responsible to you for the costs and efficiency of all the other production units. If all hands plan well during the pre-production time it becomes a situation a little like the old story of the producer being in charge of big things and his production staff in charge of little things; and he hopes that nothing big will come up. If something big *does* come up, the producer should pay quick and vigorous attention, for the problem will have passed through very good hands on its way to him. As I've said before, if the pre-production planning is sensible, careful, thorough, and cognizant of most all the elements that make up the picture, there is very little need for the producer to do more than keep a watchful check on the fulfillment of all that planning. Even then, something always comes up.

Of course contingencies arise during shooting; the best laid plans go awry in some way or another, whereupon the producer turns first to this production staff for both information and solutions. They are at the top of a chain of command and the producer is ill advised to go to any of the staff directly with problems that can be dealt with by the production manager or the assistant director or the technical advisor or the accountant or the script supervisor. To do so waters down their posture with others on the crew.

As I have said before, preparation is nine tenths of the game. And it starts with the production manager and the budget and the schedule of shooting.

I am going to go at this chapter function by function.

THE PRODUCTION MANAGER

He comes on the job first and his immediate task is to make a sequence-by-sequence breakdown of the script. There is a page of breakdown-form paper devoted to each sequence—a sequence being that which happens in one set of story circumstances, be it a quarter of a script page or five script pages. The breakdown sheet will contain a space for a scene number (every cut has a number in the script that the production manager works with). This form will have a place for the set name, the actors involved, the number of pages in the sequence, whether it is day or night, whether it is on stage or on location. It will have a space in which to indicate any special out-of-the-ordinary problem, be it a light change, the need for an earthquake effect, any special props, etc. And, finally, it will contain a synopsis of what happens within that sequence. How many breakdown pages there will be depends upon the pace and nature of the picture. A slow-paced character study might be no more than twenty-five or thirty sequences. Whereas an action/ adventure piece could very well be seventy-five, one hundred, two hundred. [See page 70 for a sample breakdown page.]

CONTINUITY BREAKDOWN

TITLE: *The Thief & The Model*   B. D. PAGE No. 38

PROD. NO. 1001?   DIRECTOR *Name*   SEQUENCE # 40

SET *Int. Barnes Cabin (Stage)*   DAY OR NIGHT D

SCENE No. 40   SCRIPT PAGES 2

SYNOPSIS:
Barnes and Bill argue about plans and over protecting Mabel

CAST	COS. NO.	ATMOSPHERE	PROPS
Barnes	3	✓	Drink materials. Jelly glass 2 Whiskey bottles
Bill	2		

BITS	SPECIAL EFFECTS ✓ Rain at windows	VEHICLES AND LIVESTOCK ✓
✓	SOUND ✓ Muffle waterfall sound.	
	MUSIC ✓	

SPECIAL NOTE:

TIME _____

The production manager then transfers the information on each one of those breakdown pages onto a separate cross-plot strip . . . 1/4 inch wide, 30 inches long. There is a "crossplot board" into which these strips tightly fit—the same 30 inches high, but 4 feet long. On the left edge of the cross-plot board will be a broader strip of cardboard with the names of the characters listed and numbered, from most important to least important. Thus a crossplot strip will indicate an actor's presence in a scene purely by number, it being alongside his name on the crossplot board. The strip will also show the scene numbers, night and/or day, on stage or location (all of these by initials . . . D,N,S,L) . . . and a very short summary running lengthwise of the strip at its bottom. [See page 72 for a sample crossplot covering just two days.]

The production manager then moves these strips about, into a tentative shooting order, one by one, according to the following standards:

    1. Get location shooting done first . . . the absurd outcome of failing to do this would be having the last three days of the "shoot" on location; then it rains . . . and you have no interior to turn to. Result: three days of idleness at, maybe, $50,000 a day. Get this risk out of the way while you have a cover set to go to (a cover set being one built well in advance in case the shooting company has to come in from the bad weather.)

    2. Go in script sequence *to* each set and stay there; while there go in script sequence *within* that set.

    3. Break the above rules only for some reason peculiar to this script: to economize on the number of pay days for certain actors or a body of extras, or a costly actor appears in

Breakdown page	10	14	16		9	17	19	38	6	4		
Day or Night	D	D	D		D	D	D	D	N			
Location or Studio	L	L	L		L	L	L	L	L			
Sequence												
No. of Pages	4/8	7/8	3 3/	4 3/4	4/8	4/8	4/8	3/8	4/8	4 4/8		

Title: *The Thief & The Model*

Director:

Producer:

Script Dated:

Character – #												
BARNES — 1		1	1	1	1	1	1	1		1		
MABEL — 2		2			1	2	2					
GORDON — 3				3								
BILL — 4		4	4			4	4					
ANNE — 5									5			
LILLIE — 6												
Bits — 7												
Extras — 8									8			
9									9			
Spec. Effects												
Stunts — 10				10								
Vehicles — 11		11										
Animals — 12			12									

Scene descriptions (bottom, read by column):
- TRAVEL TO LOCATION
- Barnes Drives up
- Barnes applies girls
- Forming a Plan
- Gordon prowling, Barnes catches
- Love Scene
- Go over tactics
- Quarrel over Mabel
- Barnes asleep - prowler
- Little girl in trouble

Int. / Ext. Barnes Cabin (column location labels)

Each narrow, vertical area represents a plastic strip that can be moved about, as the schedule is worked over, to best use the location, the cast, and that particular day of work.

E T C.

several sets and it might be cost effective to move about to shorten his engagement, or 200 extras are in the dance-hall set for one page and in the bar for three pages on another stage.

4. A black vertical strip will be in place at the end of a succession of strips which constitute a day's work in his opinion.

He will decide at this point whether or not a Second Unit is advisable in terms of travel economy for the main, First Unit of production, or, in the case of action pictures, the safety of the performers demanding stunt doubles. The Second Unit usually has a script and a book of set-up sketches in order to achieve a match with first unit plans.

And when he has finished the job of assessing the script's problems and its shooting order, as expressed by the cross-plot strips and the number of black strips he's put in indicating shooting days, he takes a monetary look at it to determine whether it is consistent with what he's been told are the budget parameters. If the producer has told the production manager that he is only going to be able to spend $3.5 million on this picture there's no point in the production manager laying out a sixty-day schedule. Still, the picture may cross-plot out in more days than the budget can stand. Now the producer steps in to help compress the schedule into fewer days, holding on to dramatic impact areas as best he can. Where do you sacrifice the least?

A practical shooting schedule in hand (on pre-printed forms filled in cross-plot order and with information from the breakdown sheets listing the work day-by-day rather than set-by-set) the production manager has the means and all the preparation necessary to make a budget. [See page 74 for a sample shooting schedule page.]

A budget is a very important document and one for

SHOOTING SCHEDULE

PROD. NO. _1001 X_ TITLE _The Thief & The Model_ _____ PAGE _7_

DIRECTOR _Name_ _____ PRODUCER _Name_ _____ ART DIR _Name_

BREAKDOWN ASST. _____ SCRIPT DATED _3-15_ _____

SCHED. DAYS _40_ START DATE _6-12_ FINISH DATE _8-6_ _____ TYPED_____

DATE	SET	PAGES	SEQ.	CAST
7-1	Int Barnes Cabin Gordon prowling, Barnes catches	4/8	19	Barnes Gordon Stunt for fight
	Int. Barnes Cabin Short Love Scene	2/8	28	Barnes Mabel
	Int. Barnes Cabin Go over battle tactics	6/8	29	Barnes Mabel Bill
	Int. Barnes Cabin Quarrel over Mabel	2	40	Barnes Bill
	Int. Barnes Cabin Barnes asleep - prowler looks	3/8	13	Barnes Extra
	Int. Barnes Cabin Little girl tells her troubles	7/8	9	Barnes Anne Lightening effect.
7-2	Ext. Open Country	2	47-50	Barnes Bill Gordon

Continued-

which you rely very much on the production manager's expertise and experience in terms of anticipating costs that the script sometimes only hints at. But his experience will tell him that if you're going to be, let's say, covering a speed boat race, you have to handle it very differently than you do two lovers out in a canoe. In the preliminary budget which he prepares soon after starting work, he will make general-allowance figures for most physical items . . . wardrobe or props or sets or dressings or special effects (these allowances will be modified, item by item, when the department head is on salary and the budget is more particularized). In manpower departments, he knows from experience how many men he will need in each department. If it's a story that takes place within twelve short hours he knows very well that he will only need one wardrobe man and one wardrobe woman because there's not much time for changing clothes. Whereas, if it's a story that takes place over a long period of time and involves many performers, it might be that he's got to beef up the wardrobe staff (and make-up staff, too) just on account of the number of changes that will take place. As I cover each of these departments in future chapters, I will be talking about how their work is budgeted and controlled. For now, I merely need to emphasize how important the production manager's work is in this preliminary budget, for it becomes a working guide as to what must be done in order to make the picture for the money that has been allowed. Again, it's like herding bees with a switch . . . fifty to a hundred in staff out there spending money, day after day.

In the studio you take this budget to management and they okay it or they say you've got to take a million dollars out of it. In independent production, as the producer, you know how much money you have to spend from the arrangements you have with your financiers. And it might be that this preliminary budget is well within the margins set by both independent financing organizations and the studio. However, it is my experience that, more often than not, the production manager, in a wish to be artistically generous to everyone, will have come in a little bit high. (Long ago I was active in budget preparation at Paramount and I formed the opinion in a short while that the head of the studio was a better budgeteer than I. He invariably set a cost limit on a given picture about ten per cent lower than my first estimate, motivating me and the production manager, no doubt.

And then the producer and the production manager must go to work on that preliminary budget and find out where to cut it. Where to cut becomes a producer's decision because there are some places that probably will not hurt the story very much to cut. There are other places that would be deadly on that story to cut. It's back to something I've said before: the producer often has to decide where to save $1,000 and where to splurge $100,000.

Along about this time in the pre-production work, another important decision comes along for the producer: shall the production be staffed with IATSE (International Alliance of Theatrical Stage Employees) Union members or go non-union? Non-union can be cheaper because, while their weekly rates may be about the same as Union scale, you can avoid some of the Union staffing, fringe benefit provisions, and manpower minimums, and job separations (nobody but full-time greensman can move plants around; a grip cannot help an electrician move a light), thus, going with a smaller crew . . . but, in the view of many, a less well-trained and less experienced crew. And, it is true that a trained and experienced crew can save money too by the speed and accuracy with which they do their work. This is a dilemma in which the production manager can help the producer with the dollar difference, but with the quality difference left in your lap. I personally believe in shooting with the IATSE crews because, ideologically speaking, a business should support and nurture its manpower pool. Fight 'em about rates, crew size, fringe benefits, but see to it that they survive. The IA has rigid standards for admission and for progress through the rating levels which, while stern and sometimes autocratic, insures a high level of performance.

After years of watching sets at work, it still amazes me when I see yet another evidence of an experienced crews' expertise and intelligent adaptability. In working a feature for Coppola's Zoetrope company, I, of course, got well acquainted with my crew . . . a group that obviously understood they were on a six-million-dollar, sixty-day picture, and therefore were careful in their selection of ways and means and things . . . fine tuning every move. Shortly after that picture's finish, I embarked on a Movie-for-Tele-vision . . . 2 1/2 million dollars and twenty-two days! Impressed as I had been with the Zoetrope crew, I hired almost all the key men to be "keys" on that TV shoot, explaining, "Now, fellas, this is a different game . . . a different pace." They just nodded. And they changed gears as smoothly as a Maserati gear-box . . . ("Into high gear, boys. Time is short") . . . far fewer selections of ways and means and things (good but less), plus abrupt, quick decisions on how to make this move or that one. Same crew, bright enough and good enough to slip into the gear that circumstances required and still do a fine job.

(I often quarrel with the IA job-protection tactics. They claim to be artists, ergo: there should be no restrictions on membership except want of talent or experience . . . not country nor city-of-birth bars.) Incidentally, if you're working out of a major studio, you don't have this choice; all studios are IATSE signatories.

Sometimes this preliminary, preparatory work will have

been done before anyone else has been assigned to the picture; you've got to have a go-ahead money figure before setting other work in motion! In other cases, the money controllers are so certain that the picture will be made that some talent (especially the director) will come aboard while the money battle is still raging.

In either case, the producer must be aware of the value of preparation time for all creative hands; day-by-day shooting costs are so high, made up as they are of space and equipment rentals, big crew and cast salaries, etc., that a few extra dollars lavished on preparation is insignificant by comparison to hold-up time on the set. In future chapters, I will be pointing out how preparation pays off for many of the top staff who are coming aboard about now, one by one, according to the urgency or size of their task for this picture.

At some appropriate time (before much money has been spent and after the cost parameters are known) the production manager will chair a staff production meeting with the producer and the director at his side. The budget and schedule will be gone over item by item, day by day, department by department, so that all hands agree on what is to be done, when, and with how much money. Since the production manager, the producer, and the director have probably had prior, meticulous planning moments with everyone on the staff, this meeting is a sort of confirmation hearing during which last-minute adjustments are judged and made.

This production meeting, when all the creative talents are together, is a good time for the producer to remind them that they must keep one another informed of their plans so that each person's work meshes sensibly with everyone else's. If out of sync, any one of seven artists can frustrate the work of the other six: the cameraman, the art director, the set decorator, the property person, wardrobe, make-up, hairdresser—each should be aware of what the others are planning. This exchange of information can take place well ahead of time, or, if circumstances dictate, at the last minute. That way, you won't face the problem of the leading woman walking onto a pink-walled apartment set wearing a pink dress . . . nor a prop man providing a story-important wrist watch to a woman wearing long sleeves (it should have been a neck-pendant watch, or short sleeves . . . they didn't talk to one another). The examples are endless. The producer must make sure that these artists exchange information—be it via sketches, concrete examples, or word of mouth.

The production manager, once shooting has started, will generally be one to five days ahead of the shooting company, making sure that the facilities necessary for those following day's shootings are in place . . . be it decorated automobiles or elephants or special wardrobe or the weather forecast for the location that comes up in a week. He tries to stay ahead as a troubleshooter. And, as I've mentioned before, he is also observant about how the set is operating and how the future days are falling in place in order to report to the producer with any problems that have to be dealt with at a higher level. He may find that he cannot get certain facilities together for the amount of money budgeted. He may find that certain important things are no longer available. In both these cases, juggle the schedule to provide time for solution. He may find that the director is demanding certain elements in the days to come that were not budgeted or not available and has to be talked out of them in some way. In the back of his mind throughout this vigilance is the budget; he will offset good news with bad to the end that, while the particulars may vary from the item to item, the total cost is right on.

The production manager's function tapers away at the end of shooting. He will, at that time, get with the accountant and make sure that all the bills are in, wrap up the financial aspect, terminate the rental arrangements that were made, and finish all the business affairs that were set in motion when the picture started.

In television, the production manager is doing all these chores simultaneously on at least three episodes: break down this one, budget that one, watch the stage on the third.

THE ASSISTANT DIRECTOR

He should come on the picture about the time that the cross-plot is being laid out because it will be his responsibility on the set to make that cross-plot work and to make the schedule that comes out of that cross-plot work day by day.

His feet are really in two tubs of hot water. The first demanding that he run the set in such a way that its mechanics do not intrude on the director's mind as that busy man seeks performance and visual realization. And the other heated foot is in the matter of trying to lead all hands to a finish of that day's work on schedule, and, with whatever time there is to spare, anticipate the problems of tomorrow so that it too can go smoothly.

He is the manager of the operation of the set. He is following the will of the director, but is the one who has to make it all work smoothly. He is the one who has to foresee that the actress working on the set at this moment has a very quick change of wardrobe coming up and, if they're really going to maintain their day's pace properly, he must make sure that the wardrobe people are alert and ready to help her make that change. Or that the next shot will require a car to drive through. Is the car ready? He must see that coming. Or when to call a break for a meal . . . union regulations make a goof here expensive.

And he is also the set watchdog for the producer in terms of being aware of problems that arise that are beyond his franchise to deal with and a troublesome thing for the director to face. He gets to the producer who must then deal with whatever teset problems may be.

The assistant director also schedules the day-to-day life of the actors. By that I mean, performers all value their moments and times of relaxation and spend it in their dressing rooms, or in the corner of the set, relaxing. The assistant director is the one who has to foresee that in five minutes or ten minutes or two minutes that actor or actress will be needed on the set and alert the actor to the need. A bad assistant will call actors far ahead of their need and cause ill will . . . an unnecessary enervation. In short, his conduct toward the actors has a lot to do with the set running smoothly as far as the performers are concerned. The producer must be sensitive to the assistant director's efficiency, in terms of both money and smooth operations. The grapevine from set to producer's office works well and he will hear of both fault and triumph without having to stand set-side.

The assistant director is the *director* of the extras in the scene, especially in crowd scenes. The director's eyes and mind are focused on the leading players. The behavior of the crowd on the sidewalk, the eaters at the restaurant, the spectators at the crew race, is up to the assistant director and his helpers. The director will have generalized about what effect he wants from the extras; in following these vagaries, the assistant is training to be a director some day.

This diplomatic traffic manager has an assistant called a second assistant director, who is largely a mechanical aid. He is sent to the corner of the set in order to get the actor; he fills out the production report for the day, with the help of the script supervisor's notes, saying how many pages they covered and who worked for how long and what time lunch was called—this is a very mechanical report which the second assistant prepares at the end of each day. [See page 84 and page 85 for a sample production report.] The second assistant probably started as a Directors' Guild trainee; now, after that internship, he can often prove that the First AD can be in two places at once.

THE ACCOUNTANT

In a studio there is an accounting department with a great deal of accounting machinery surrounding the production of a picture. On an independent production or most television productions there is a single person to whom the production manager sends all the bills, who handles payroll, who keeps track of expenses to the point of even knowing that each day is costing X amount of money. He's very important to the producer in terms of finding out whether the budget goals and reality are matching up. All the picture's expenses go through his hands. Thus, he is a listening post from whom the producer hears only when there's trouble. I've spent many a picture without having had to bother the accountant nor him bother me. Except when things go wrong dollarwise.

TECHNICAL ADVISOR

Some pictures, but not all, require an advisor who understands the milieu in which the picture is made. It's a picture that might take place in a factory, let's say, or it's about airplanes, or is deep into the problems of the medical profession, or it takes place on a farm. You need somebody on hand who knows how the farm works, how a hospital works, how a factory works so that the director will be able to make sure that his picture is realistic and is accurate. (This source of accurate information must also be available to the various artists who need to be exact in their work— art director, prop man, wardrobe, make-up, hairdress). Once again there is a chore being done here that the producer seldom hears about unless something goes wrong. I've had occasion to hear from technical directors who have told me that the director of the picture was playing ducks and drakes with the truth for dramatic effect. That left me in the position of finding out whether I'd rather be accurate or dramatic. And quite often it can be worked out. Sometimes accuracy is not really all that important. Sometimes the dramatic effect can be fully realized in such a way that it doesn't play with the truth.

THE SCRIPT SUPERVISOR

Traditionally, a woman's job because, in former times, before small tape dictating machines and computers, short-hand skills were mandatory and the job was a natural promotion for studio secretaries. It is perhaps the most meticulous job on the set and the most difficult in a great many ways because the script supervisor is responsible for detailing in her copy of the script (which she duplicates for the director and especially for the editor) an account of every take from every angle that the camera assumes. In other words, every foot of film exposed is accounted for in her script, even that which, for whatever reason, is not printed. She notes where the camera is, who's in the shot and what they say as compared to the script dialogue, whether that was a print or not, and whether it was incomplete . . . at what point in the scene did it stop and what happened to cause it not to be a print. The need for this sort of meticulous accounting comes up on two differ-ent occasions.

WEATHER { FAIR / CLOUDY / RAIN / SOUND STAGE / STUDIO LOT / LOCATION }
No. Days Estimated

DAILY PRODUCTION REPORT

DAILY PRODUCTION REPORT

Date _7-1_

No. of Days on Picture Including Today					
Holidays	Idle	Rehearsals	Retake	WORK	TOTAL
1	⌐	1	⌐	40	42

Title _The Thief & The Model_   Director _Name_

Production No. _10012_ Date Started _6-12_ Est. Finish Date _8-6_ Status _on Schedule_

Set _Int. Barnes Cabin_

Location _Studio_

Shooting Call _8-_ First Shot _8^40_ Lunch From _12_ Til _12 45_ Supper From _—_ Til _—_ Midnite Meal _—_

Crew Call _7-_ Wrap _5^10_ Lunch From _12_ Til _12 45_ Supper From _—_ Til _—_ Midnite Meal _—_

FOR REMARKS AND EXPLANATIONS OF DELAYS, SEE OTHER SIDE.   Extra Bus Arr. at Studio _____ Crew Bus Arr. at Studio _____

Script	Scenes	Pages	MINUTES		SETUPS	
SCENES IN SCRIPT	161	104 3/4	Prev.	37 1/2	Prev.	134
ADD OR DELETE			Today	3	Today	8
TAKEN PREV		35 1/2	Total	40 1/2	Total	142
TAKEN TODAY		4 1/8				
TAKEN TO DATE		43 5/8				
TO BE TAKEN		61 1/8	WILDTRACKS, OTHER: X			

SCENES SHOT TODAY:
#19 Gordon prowls, Barnes catches
28 Love Scene - Barnes - Mabel
40 Barnes - Bill quarrel over Mabel
13 Prowler looks in on Barnes
9 Anne tells Barnes her troubles

CAST—Contract and Day Players Worked—W Started—S / Rehearsal—R Hold—H / Finished—F On Call—C	W S R / H F C	LV. STUDIO	MAKEUP	ON SET	DISMISS SET	ARRIVE STUDIO	REMARKS
Simon West	W		730	8-	5^10		
Adam Jones	W		730	8-	9^45		
Joanna Winter	W		8-	9^30	12-		
Sam Martin	W		8^30	10	3^30		
Marian Shell (Anne)	WF		3^30	4	5^10		
Ben Mitchell	H						
Lillian Forest	H						

ATMOSPHERE, WELFARE WORKERS, AND SIDELINE MUSICIANS										LUNCH DURA.	SUPPER DURA.	MIDNITE DURA.	
NO.	CALL	DISMISS SET	ARR. STUDIO	OUT WORK	RATE	ADJ. TO	FLAT ADJ.	M.P.V.					
1	3-	4-			Mini								

PICTURE NEGATIVE			INSERTS / PICKUPS	

	PRINT	N. G.	WASTE
USED PREV.	18,720	PREV. 32,111	PREV. 1401
USED TODAY.	1,835	TODAY 2115	TODAY 112
USED TO DATE	20,559	TO DATE 34,226	TO DATE 1413
TOTAL USED TO DATE			

PROD. NO.	10012	NEGATIVE	
SERIES		PRINT	
START TIME		N. G.	
FIN. TIME		WASTE	
TOTAL TIME		TOTAL USED	
SCENE NOS.			

Report ABSENSES on Account of Illness of Any Member of the Cast or Staff

NAMES	REMARKS

Remarks and Explanation of Delays

Staff and Crew

- Director
- Asst. Directors-2
- Script Supervisor
- Dialogue Director
- Cameraman
- Operator
- Assistants-2
- Still Man
- Mixer
- Recorder
- Mike Boom Man
- Cable Man
- Playback Operator
- Propmaster
- Asst. Propmaster
- Key Grip
- 2nd Co. Grip
- Crane Dolly Grip
- Crane Grip
- Extra Co. Grips-4
- Craft Service
- Greensman
- S. B. Painter
- Gaffer
- Best Boy
- Lamp Operators - 6
- Generator Man
- 40 Man
- Special Effects Man- Rain
- Makeup Artist
- Hair Stylist
- Body Makeup Woman
- Wardrobe Man
- Wardrobe Woman
- Wranglers, Trainers, Handlers
- Whistleman

Miscellaneous Crew

- First Aid Man
- Fireman
- Police
- AHA Man

Equipment

- Camera Car
- Insert Car
- Blue Goose with Sound
- Sound Truck
- Electrical Truck
- Generator
- Prop Truck
- Sp. EFX Truck
- Grip Truck
- Horse Wagon Truck
- Honey Wagon   D.R.
- Water Truck
- Busses
- Stretchout: 11 Pass, 14 Pass, 18 Pass
- Station Wagon
- Misc. Cars
- Picture Cars _____
- Wagons
- Horses
- Cattle
- Other Animals
- Cameras
- Cranes – Large ☐ Medium ☐ Small ☒
- Hyster for High Shot
- Lunches # 48 Dinners # _____ Midnite # _____
- Crab Dolly
- Misc. Equip.

PICTURE CARS DETAIL

No.	Description

Producer Namp

Director

Asst. Dir.

Prod. Mgr.

Camerman

Mixer

Assistant Director

SIGNED BY: Unit Manager

Number one, on the set itself, when the director, now in a new angle, turns to the script supervisor and says, "How did John read that line the last time?" Because it has to match. Or, the director will turn to the script supervisor and say, "When John went through that door three days ago did he have his tie on or his tie off?"

Number two, when the editor is working with the film, he also has a word file of every foot available to him. Perhaps he will find in the script supervisor's notes that there is an outtake that was not printed that could very well help him out of a problem. Because the script editor's notes indicate that the shot was cut well past the screen moment that the editor needs to have in the clear, he orders a reprint, and there's the close-up that he needs or the line of dialogue he's missing. In short, the script supervisor provides a history for every shot that is taken. Thus the producer can read, when in need, this report as an inventory of every foot available for the post-production process. [See pages 88 and 89 for a page of a script supervisor's notes and a page of marked script.]

The script supervisor keeps little notes for her own reference about wardrobe, props, hairdos, etc., so that when problems of matching from one set to another come up, there's an answer in hand. The craftsmen in charge of those elements have kept meticulous matching notes too; the script supervisor's are just a double check.

The script supervisor participates very importantly in another aspect of the producer's responsibility: how long a picture does this script indicate? How many minutes? Ninety minutes is about par for a motion picture. Does this particular project warrant going longer, thus risking trying the audience's patience? Is it a brisk comedy or high-tempo melodrama that should be shorter? Well, both matters can be settled later in the editorial process by shooting fully, then trimming and deleting. But the costs of shooting unneeded material must be considered; so the script supervisor reads the script and times it . . . guessing at action pacing, reading the lines at a guess tempo. An experienced script supervisor will be amazingly accurate; sufficiently so that a producer can cut sequences or have new sequences written before shooting for an ideal length with comparative security. Then, as the picture shoots, the script supervisor adjusts her guess readings to the actuality of the set, and informs the interested parties—producer, director, editor. Then, if necessary, adjustments are made. Adjustments in script bulk are seldom made during shooting because each sequence will play a bit differently . . . slower . . . faster . . . (compensating, over all) . . . and it would be a mistake to tamper with a good script structure. However, if timings are surprising, a director might decide to pick up the pace or slow it down.

This matter of script timing becomes very important, and sometimes stressful, in TV production because of the rigid time limits on broadcasts: about twenty-three-plus minutes playing time for a half-hour show, and about forty-eight-plus minutes for an hour show. The producer and director have to keep close watch on how the script is timing out. Overlength can be trimmed down (somehow or other), but if the cut is short the project is faced with shooting added scenes and the expense thereof. As an example, director Robert Florey was early in his second day on a three-day shoot of a "Twilight Zone" episode when the script supervisor warned him that the leading man, Richard Conte, was clipping his way through the dialogue at the rate of about forty seconds a page: we were headed for a twenty-minute episode. Charles Beaumont rushed in, wrote two extra scenes, and Mr. Florey extended Suzanne Lloyd's dance in the funhouse. We made it; vigilance had paid off.

| 40. | 7/1 | MTR 40 mm. | WS over foot of bed, DOLLY INTO MWS Barnes. Two shot Barnes and Bill when Bill stops, Barnes stands. |

1 - 0:10 ngc
2 - 0:14 BB walked into C.
3 - 0:21 B said "finicky timing".
4 - 0:31 H
5 - 0:32 P

| 40a | 7/1 | MS 27 mm. | Across foot of bed to BB, PAN his pacing. B rises into a 2-shot. |

1 - 0:30 S. lost BB.
2 - 1:01 H. Almost it.
3 - 1:31 H.
4 - 1:01 BB stumbled
5 - 1:30 P.
6 - 1:35 P.

| 40b | 7/1 | C.U. 75 mm. | B. lying back in bed. |

1 - 0:13 Shaky start
2 - 0:45 P.

| 40c | 7/1 | MS 40 mm. | B goes to mix drinks. BB argues on. |

1 - 0:58 C. ngc
2 - 0:19 NGS Bottle noises over dialogue.
3 - 0:45 H
4 - 0:58 P

| 40d | 7/1 | C. U. 75 mm. | BB angry. |

1 - 0:12 C.
2 - 0:14 H.
3 - 0:11 P.

Glossary:

MTR - Master Shot	ngc - no good for camera	B - Barnes
MS - Medium Shot	ngs - no good for sound	BB- Bill
WS - Wide Shot	I - incomplete scene	
CU - Close up	C - complete scene	
OTS - Over shoulder	H - hold	
	P - print	

| On Camera | Not on Camera | End of Shot | Shot goes on to next page. |

40. INT. BARNES CABIN - DAY - RAIN AT WINDOWS -

Barnes is lying comfortably on the room's one cot, and
Bill is pacing back and forth, looking out one window
at the worrisome weather, then the other.

                    BARNES
You've got to calm down a bit.

                    BILL
How can I? This is dangerous...
for Mabel, especially.

                    BARNES
If this caper is goin' to work,
you've got to forget Mabel.

Bill stops his pacing, angrily facing Barnes.

                    BILL
Forget that girl?

                    BARNES
          (calmly, reasonably)
What we're trying for takes
delicate timing...people being
exactly where they belong, when
they belong...with the right gun.
          (he pauses)
Can't do that with your mind
on the lady.

                    BILL
          (resuming his pacing)
Okay. You're right. But...
well, it's hard...she's...

Barnes rises quickly from the cot, and goes to the little
dining table where there are two glasses and two bottles.

                    BARNES
Sam's agreed to help us out.

                    BILL
          (turning, excited)
That's good news...for once,

                    BARNES
Have a drink.

                    BILL
Let's go over the plans again...

                                        CONTINUED -

It is not my objective herein to tell how a picture is made, but only how a producer has to conduct himself during it's making . . . knowing, as he must, what is going on, and precisely who is doing what. In the matter of the production staff, which we have just been discussing, their work is very important to what the producer must accomplish. And with a good production manager, a good assistant director, a good accountant, a good script supervisor, he will have little more to do than review their work from time to time and when it's completed. The producer does not participate in the making of the breakdown or the crossplot, nor the making of the budget. But he has to check out all of these elements to make sure that they conform to his intentions as far as the picture is concerned. Again, there are functions that the producer has to be aware are going on but which he does not have to be on top of every minute, nor know how to do himself.

On the following page are three sample budgets with different cost goals and shooting schedules. I omit the forty-sixty million dollar budget as illegible to the sane mind.

Script dated_____   Start Date_____
Script Length_____pgs.   Studio Days_____
Prod. #_____   Location Days_____
Date:_____   Travel Days_____
Title:_____

	20 Days, M.O.W. Budget	48 Days, Modest Budget	60 Days, High Budget
Story	10,000.	50,000.	125,000
Director	155,000.	344,000.	800,000.
Cast	325,000.	427,800.	4,850,000.
Extras	67,500.	16,500.	278,000.
Total above line	557,500.	838,300.	6,053,000.
Production staff	211,200.	303,400.	575,000
Sets & Dress	222,000.	262,000.	2,100,000.
Props & Prop Man	88,000.	156,500.	385,000.
Cameraman	88,000.	167,700.	442,000.
Grip, Set Oper.& Elec.	131,000.	214,650.	677,000.
Prod. Sound	24,000.	36,500.	122,000.
Special Effects	31,000.	350,000.	110,000.
Wardrobe	75,000.	43,600.	338,000.
Makeup & Hairdress	30,000.	21,000.	170,000.
Publicity	5,000.	15,000.	24,000.
Transportation	170,000.	295,000.	988,000.
Location	228,000.	436,000.	484,500.
Studio & Equip.	25,000.	67,500.	595,500.
Film & Processing	38,500.	143,500.	239,000.
Total Prod.	1,366,700.	2,512,350.	7,250,000.
Editorial	134,000.	171,000.	645,000.
Music	68,750.	300,000.	400,000.
Post-prod. Sound	53,500.	94,500.	442,000.
Post-prod. Lab.	88,000.	106,000.	130,000.
Total, Post-prod.	344,250.	671,500.	1,617,000
Miscellaneous:			
Insurance	100,000.	161,000.	290,000.
Fringes, etc.	141,000.	161,000.	1,936,000.
Gen'l Expense	65,000.	329,500.	295,000.
Total, Misc. Exp.	306,000.	651,000.	2,521,000.
TOTAL COSTS	2,574,450.	4,673,650.	17,441,000.

7
SET DESIGN AND
SET DECORATION

I am writing of these two artists and their ways of working in the same chapter because they are really a closely paired team whose expertise provides the workspace for the players, be it an exterior on location, an exterior set in the studio, a real interior on location, or an interior set in the studio.

(First, let me clear up some confusion about nomenclature: the terms "production designer," "art director," "set designer," each name designates one single function, but are separated on the screen nowadays by a current love for titles. If the burden placed upon set design and construction is light, there will only be a production designer; if getting the sets thought out and up is a little more complex, there will be an art director as well; if it gets really tough, a third party will come on—the set designer.)

Whichever he chooses to call himself, this artist is basically an architect, dealing with the look of exterior and interior spaces. The set decorator, in coordination with the art director, furnishes the sets appropriately. The difference between these artists and the man who builds a house or a shopping center, or the man who helps you select the furniture for your living room, is that they are dealing in story-telling illusions . . . impressions of reality . . . or unreality.

The producer must understand what these artists and their staffs are capable of doing (note: not how they do it) in order to administer their work, look over their preliminary plans and sketches, then their finished work. And then applaud or ask for further effort.

Again, both they and the director and you must agree on the artistic intentions of the script . . . the "tone" or "look" that is wanted for the finished picture. Is it grim realism, calling for dirty hand marks on the sagging doors and broken bricks on the walls, or is it romance wherein the boy and girl live an idyllic love life in a Paris garret with a view of roof tops and moonsets? Are the characters rich or poor . . . having good taste or bad . . . young or old? Is it a matter-of-fact picture calling for in-focus realism . . . or a bit mistily out of this world? Is it a period piece wherein authenticity commands severe guidelines, or is it modern, giving free rein for the look to contribute to character and story telling? Whichever, these two men and their aides contribute in a major way (along with the cameraman) to conveying these moods to the audience.

As in real life, the architect starts, before the decorator, by studying the script, participating in the budget process as far as sets are concerned, then meeting with the director and the producer. He will have done his research, which is necessary whether the picture is modern or deeply set in the past. Even a "today" picture calling for a jail corridor and cell, or a beauty parlor, has to be researched for today's accuracy and for filmic ideas. He's prepared. "How do you want this to look?" The art director will generally answer with rough sketches illustrating his ideas, plus floor plans showing dimensions, how many walls, how high, what color. Ergo: a "design" for the production; thus the title.

To facilitate this communication of ideas, the art director will often afford a sketch artist and even a model maker; this work is not akin to a blueprint that often suffices for house building. It is a two-dimensional, and, in the case of a model, three-dimensional, visualization of the art director's plans for the look of the picture. Both of these, sketch and model, remove much of the anxiety that a director feels about how sets are going to match up to his visual plans. Sketches and models are especially useful when the look wanted is outside ordinary human experience: science fiction, dream worlds, outer space, 2010 A.D.,etc. [See pages 95 and 96.]

When agreement is reached here, the probable costs have to be equated with the budget. The production manager, as we have seen, has put in a considerate guess figure; that figure is inevitably too low for the art director. Whereupon the juggling starts: can this less important set be built for less? Does this one need to be so elaborate? With tears in his eyes, the art director will often ask the producer or the production manager if some money can't be taken out of props or some other account; if sets are where some measurable story strength lies, all hands will try to find some money somewhere.

The producer should know of one major distinction between art directors; some are very stern realists, feeling that the only way to convey to an audience the locale of this scene is to duplicate it in the way that the audience has seen it: a brick wall is made of brick, doors have hardware that works and locks that lock, most sets have four walls; if the story is about rich people, then their living room is big and tall. This is a fail-safe, but expensive, method that has the virtue of letting the director change his mind: he wants the enraged actor to beat on the brick wall with a baseball bat instead of on the floor; he wants the angered leading lady to turn the key in the bedroom door against her husband rather than bend over and weep; he wants to reverse the

The script dictated a scene in which the leading man dreams that, instead of playing ordinary chess with his crusty neighbor, he physically fights him on a giant chess board. What size should the squares be? What size the chessmen? Joe Griffith sketched this to guide all hands to a mutually satisfactory solution.

Illustration: Joe Griffith, Concept Artist, *Time After Time.*

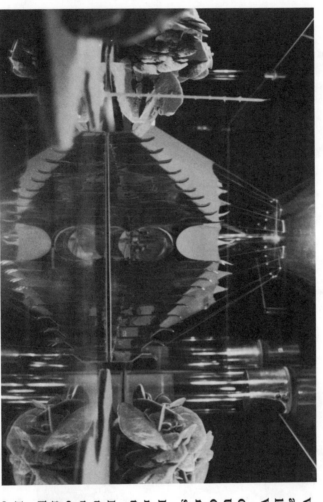

What would a gambling casino and night club on a distant star look like? Like nothing in Las Vegas?

Glen Larson, producer of the Universal series, "Battlestar Galactica," turned to his Art Director, Dale Allan Pelton, and said "What?"

Here is a picture of the design model on which Pelton based the final set.

Its style undoubtedly helped the set decorator and, probably, the wardrobe designer . . . everyone . . . to establish a "look" for that star, its people, and its buildings.

Photo: Model of a gambling casino for "Battlestar Galactica" designed by Art Director Dale Allan Pelton.

camera against the wall, for whatever reason, that was not anticipated; he wants the rich family to wander all over their huge living room as they argue.

Conversely, there is the art director who is an impressionist . . . and cheaper. A brick wall is flat-painted on plywood (as planned, the camera is not going to be within twenty feet of it); the doors are visual information only; given a matching-color flat with a picture hanging on it, you don't need a fourth wall (or maybe even a third one) for a reverse shot at Horace. He will build a rich living-room set that seems to be forty feet deep, but will really be only twenty-five because the back fifteen feet is in increasingly smaller perspective (the fireplace, way in the back, may be only one-and-a-half feet high and two-feet wide; of course, no actor may walk into that miniaturized portion of the set).

All art directors must use their ingenuity about finding sets that are standing around the studio (or available elsewhere in town, for that matter). They also must be aware of set units that are stored here and there . . . a fireplace, an elevator, a curved stairway . . . you'd be surprised at what gets stored away. For instance, one of the main reasons that I chose to shoot "The Twilight Zone" at the MGM studios was that company's life-long policy of never throwing anything away . . . props, wardrobe items, set dressing, set units . . . extensive back lot exteriors . . . lakes, small-town streets, big-town streets, Andy Hardy's small-town residential streets, railroad stations, tanks of water, prisons. It was ideal for an anthology series that would require something different every four days. Rod Serling could scarcely think up a locale that we couldn't find right on the premises; as a matter of fact, he often got ideas from strolling the stages or the back lot, where he would encounter a park with a carousel . . . then a riverboat. It was a Pandora's box.

Much smaller studios are ideal for their compactness

when a series or a movie needs less space and fewer exterior facilities.

More and more, nowadays, pictures and TV are shot on locations in real circumstances . . . office, home, street. There, the art director's job is to adapt something already standing to his needs: the standing house is a beaut', but it looks fresh and new, whereas the picture needs an air of neglect; well, a little harmless coal dust and some washable oil will fix that. On interiors, he often tries to find a . . . living room, if you will, that is larger than the picture needs but whose largeness provides working room for the crew; a little camera jockeying and the audience will never know how big the room really is.

Like every other artist on the picture, this set designer can contribute both to the mood and to the characterizations. It's a dark and serious picture: the windows are small, letting in little light; the doors are of dark oak, thick. It's a cheerful piece about healthy, out-going people: sunlight floods the set, the colors are bright. The leading man in whose living quarters the audience spends some time, is haughty, reclusive: the set is in fussy detail, meticulous. The leading actress is an extroverted sex symbol: her bedroom is bouffant, golden in trim, fussy in window treatment. [See page 99.]

For many years, Cedric Gibbons was in charge of all the sets that were built for MGM pictures and, in accordance with Louis B. Mayer's dictum that the audience did not go to pictures to be depressed, but rather to be cheered up by what life had to offer, Gibbons ran a department that never built a gloomy set; a secretary's apartment was a little gem of good taste and the best ingredients; a businessman's office gave one ambitions to rise in the world. And Mr. Gibbons was very good at it; Metro's sets were the pride of that studio. It was a romantic era, believing in (and expect-

Here's the sex symbol's boufant bedroom for the I.T.C. movie *Poor Little Rich Girl*... about Barbara Hutton. Notice the minute detail that set decorator Robin Peyton put there for Farrah Fawcett to react to.

Both you and I would tiptoe into this room.

Photo: Courtesy of ITC Entertainment Group, Inc., Set Decorator, Robin Peyton.

ing to have) the good life, ultimately . . . and Mr. Gibbons showed them what it would be like. I tell this to remind you of what strong impressions an art director can leave with an audience. Use him well.

While I am into stories, I should tell about a famous and very talented art director who finally got to direct because some producer reasoned that, if a man could be so sensitive to storytelling as to build such sets, he should direct. This fine artist never rose to any eminence at all as a director and went back to what he did best. His explanation: "Having got the 'look' of the picture right, then I had to maneuver these people around . . . actors . . . through the sets. Beats me. They're impossible!" A general observation: good directors are hard to find and you can't tell where they'll come from.

Next on the payroll and immediately hand-in-glove with the art director is the set decorator. And a great deal of the set's impact is in his hands, for the same bedroom can be furnished as the sleeping place of a "messpot" . . . or a fashion plate . . . or a drug addict . . . or a hooker. Naturally, the decorator has read the script and done the necessary research (how is a pet hospital furnished?) and conspired with the art director; there'll be no outright dumb mistakes . . . but the decoration could be bland and contribute less to the storytelling than it should. But, pushed a little, it can work wonders; the producer should consistently see sets before they are shot, then draw in other opinions if he thinks any one of the sets falls short of the best that can be done. [See page 101.]

I was very lucky on the "The Twilight Zone" in that the head of the set decorators at MGM liked the scripts that he saw coming out of Rod's mill and decided that we merited the best he could offer; so I had Keogh Gleason (just off *Gigi*) for the first season and part of the second. I remember that an actor walked onto the set that was to be his office

The decorator on *War of the Roses*, Anne McCulley, faced a unique challenge—she had to decorate a luxurious living room in such a way that a very destructive husband/wife donnybrook/brawl would show visually and compellingly. And this is what she did. Notice the clutter of rich (and very fragile) detail—a chess set on a table with fancy chairs alongside, breakfront cupboards with vases on top, knick-knacks galore, mantle decorations, drapes, etc., etc. When the fight was over...it showed!

War of the Roses © 1989 Twentieth Century Fox Film Corp. All rights reserved.

and said, "Y'know I've been thinking about this character I'm supposed to be and this office is perfect . . . it sharpens my notion of him."

Gleason worked on the theory that you overdressed, first, then brought it down. That didn't mean he wasn't selective. The excess that he brought to the stage was all on target; but, now, how much did you need to make the point? So he'd decorate a set to the nines, pull out what he knew did not go with another piece that was more important, then start juggling. I've watched him do it, not knowing how he was making his selection and, when it was finished, it was right on the button. Once, a script called for a deserted loft that Gleason argued could be made to look more desolate with some single barren object in it. He brought a choice to the set: a big packing crate, a broken bicycle, three messy artists' easels, a bundle of newspapers, and a standing stuffed bear. He was right; his choice, the lonely bear, spoke of the life that had been lived before in that loft, and its present desertedness, better than emptiness itself.

Naturally, the director has an important hand in how a final, dressed set looks. He's been directing this picture in his mind's eye for days . . . weeks; often wondering how the set could be made to help him tell the story. The ideas are exchanged back and forth. The producer silently watches this idea factory and gloats at the wisdom he's shown in picking such a bunch.

The set decorator doesn't have to buy much; every movie center has rental houses full of furniture, pictures, lamps, clocks, beds, etc. He has to budget the rental thereof if his studio (or lack of one) can't fill his needs. At MGM, "The Twilight Zone" crew seldom had to go off the lot for anything; there was one of the most remarkable collections of set elements, furnishings, wardrobe, props, wigs, what-have-you the cinema world has ever known . . . mostly gone now under the auctioneer's hammer.

In this budget account is a sketch artist. If a set is in any way out of the ordinary, or its elements are being argued over, the producer should be sure that a sketch artist's talents are brought in to settle matters. "Here's a visualization of what it will look like. Okay?"

A sketch artist's work helps coordinate the over-all look of the picture. Every set and location can be graphically visualized: Do you need a dark set somewhere just to change the visual pace for a few minutes? So as not to be in one apartment after another, should one of the cast live in a detached house? Might this scene work better on an open location?

If the director is willing to be tied down to an exact plan of how he will shoot the picture, a sketch artist can do quick cartoons of every set-up in the picture. There are some directors who insist on a shot-by-shot set of sketches in order to get their own thoughts in order. The producer who is at all uncertain of his director's skills at long-range planning may well insist on a sketch-run of the picture; it pins people down and it helps the budget process stay on course. You pin 'em up on a wall and you can "see" the whole picture. Its called a "storyboard." [See page 104-107.]

Good model makers are available from the big-picture miniature effects area, where they make most of their money. Once in a while, however, a model will put a knotty problem into a plainer perspective. Say that your picture is about spelunking: you may need a model of the proposed cave set (or sets) so that the director, and the audience, will be clear about where the actors are from scene to scene, and the relationship between the cave units can be made sensible. It's easy to follow a cast through a house, or an office building, but through a cave, or a space ship, or a fun house? Better have a model or two.

**EXT. Hollywood
Reno Restaurant**

Closer

Storyboard by John Mann from Storyboards, Inc.

Medium Shot—
Ted and Carol
meet.

Dissolve to: Cocktail Glass as ice cube falls in—follow glass to Ted/Carol Booth.

PAN →

Two Shot—
Ted and Carol
TED
Harvey is After us.

Storyboard by John Mann from Storyboards, Inc.

C.U. Carol
CAROL
How did that happen?
Where is . . . ?

C.U. Ted
TED
He's here in town.

Two Shot—Ted and Carol.
He points his finger at her
sharply
TED
. . . and you led him to us!

C.U. Carol—Shocked
CAROL
It couldn't be . . .

Storyboard by John Mann from Storyboards, Inc.

PULL OUT

PAN

Two Shot—Ted and
Carol.
      TED
You don't think so.

Pull out and Pan to
Harvey listening—
follow him to
phone.

C.U. Harvey.
     HARVEY
I found 'em.

Storyboard by John Mann from Storyboards, Inc.

All these artists/craftsmen are proud of their work and their artistic self-sufficiency; they are good at what they do and are not about to indicate otherwise by pleading for help. It behooves a good producer to drop in once in a while and ask, "Everything okay?"

The actual physical construction of the set is in the hands of a construction foreman and his aides . . . painters, carpenters, plasterers, etc. But the art director manages that work in much the same way that an architect would the construction of a house or an office building. Having provided explicit plans, the art director will follow through, making sure that everything is correctly done and that revisions are not necessary, and that all is on budget. And it's not always just a matter of rooms and offices. [See page 109-112.]

On a distant location, an art director's job gets very tough because there is no construction foreman nor department in place. He has to whip up his own staff from the craftsmen available in that city, who may or may not understand the flimsy nature of a paper-thin wall. Often there will be a pool of competence if the city is big enough to originate some stage productions. Aware of these difficulties, the producer and production manager must arrange for the art director to have extra head-start time at a distant location.

In summary: it should be clear that the art director and the set decorator make a major contribution to the look of the picture. Is it moody and atmospheric? Is it bright and cheerful? Is it crisp, like a newspaper photograph? Is it lyrical? These artists can give the picture any one of these; they may do it intuitively . . . or may have to be asked.

This is what is needed for a Jeep to drive through, bog down, and work its way out when the stream starts to overflow . . .

Problem: Cannot use a natural location because the crew has to regulate the water flow, take after take.

Solution: Design and decorate a set that meets the dramatic needs, make it look naturally believeable—rocks, trees, water.

Photo: Art Director—Alan Rodrick Jones. Set Decorator—Robin Peyton. Produced by A&R Group for CME Advertising.

Find an airplane hangar. Put in some false ground-contour bases, and some tree bases . . .

Then cover the ground-contour lines, and build a little waterfall out of Styrofoam.

Put in the big trees . . . add foliage to the smaller trees . . .

Fill in the foliage. And you've got the set shown on page 109.

Finally, a producer must get used to seeing what is left after all the hard work on a set is over. This is the way a day's shooting left a doctor's-office set.

Set Decorator Robin Peyton took this picture: he was at first outraged and then able to laugh at it.

8
PROPS AND THE
PROPERTY MAN

"Whatever the performers handle" is a pretty good definition of props. The carpet on the floor is set decoration unless Antony is going to roll Cleopatra up in it, then it's a prop because it probably has to be special in some way . . . thin, heavy, cool. A brass lamp is decoration unless someone is going to throw it, then it's a prop because it has to appear solid but should break harmlessly on contact with the leading man's head. "Anything that moves on the set, except the actors, is a prop." All animals, boats, airplanes, cars, even the food in a restaurant setting.

Producer, remember that the prop man can contribute to characterization, to period color, or to the substantiation of a story premise or condition that isn't going to be spelled out. I remember a picture whose believability depended on the fact that this big-city attorney's home was in the country suburbs (or he couldn't conveniently have this torrid love affair with a city girl) . . . and the one time you saw his wife she was driving a station wagon! A small touch, but a telling one. Often, one's overall impression of what has been going on is made up of a lot of small touches from this professional, then that one.

The guy's rich; he's got a Gucci valise.

The woman is a street-drunk; she's got a bottle in a paper bag.

It pays to be patient with the prop department, and give them good preparation time for research; especially in a period picture like Hamlet, or a futuristic/outer-space picture where inventive ingenuity takes time, or in a "today" picture . . . what kind of guns are the thugs carrying these days? The props contribute greatly to the audience's perception that they are actually there . . . they feel it.

This man's prop box should be called a "wonder box" because of its infinite variety of "who'da thunk it" items. I have known directors who had a side game of trying to ask for something that props could not find in its 3'x5'x6' series of drawers, hangers, and cubbyholes: sewing needles, whistles, kiddie toys, bandage tape, eyeglasses, crutches, books . . . well, you won't catch him out of anything very often.

Like all department heads, the prop man will have a "guess" budget from the production manager that is adjusted when his breakdown is gone over carefully. And he has to stay within it.

Dealing productively with this talented man may seem a self-evident procedure, but, considering what he can contribute, don't forget to do it. Check the tires!

One adversarial note of warning: check the eyeglasses. Most every prop man I've ever worked with supplies eyeglasses with plain glass in them that reflects the lights that the player faces most unrealistically and, quite often, denies the audience a look at the player's eyes, where a lot of the drama is played. Insist on non-reflective, coated lenses or curved cuts that impede the player's vision only slightly.

9

THE CAMERAMAN
aka Cinematographer, or
Director of Photography

George Clemens was just about the most important man on "The Twilight Zone" set. He had been the cameraman on "The Schlitz Playhouse" which Bill Self produced and for which I had been the story editor. Self, the CBS executive in charge of "Twilight Zone" matters, picked me to produce and Clemens to photograph; that was all that he insisted on. As story editor I was not too much aware of Clemens' work, though it wasn't but a few days into "Twilight Zone" production that I realized that his talents and Rod's view of storytelling were a marriage made in film heaven. We did not have a lot of preproduction time together, but George reacted to the three scripts that we had in hand ahead of time in a way that hyped me into an almost ecstatic certainty that we had the right man. He was quiet, self-assured, and seemed to understand exactly what those scripts were getting at; they moved him in a certain way and he intended . . . firmly intended . . . to help move audiences in the same way. Real, but off-center. As Arlen Schumer says in his new book, *Visions from The Twilight Zone*, ". . . looking at the world through a jaundiced eye." (Schumer goes on to credit Clemens with responding to our dramatic material with very advanced "filmic surrealism" . . .

photography midway between real and shadow.)

Now, that is what a producer wants: a cameraman who grasps the point and clearly sees a way to use his talents and his machine to make it come off on the screen. Like many crafts that are based on complex machinery or processes, some practitioners of it are good mechanics (even brilliant) and some few are artists as well (a lithographer or an upholsterer or a gardener may be either). Clemens not only knew the tools of his trade but how to use them artistically for our story's benefit.

And, believe me, that tool . . . a motion picture camera . . . is complex. Forgetting artistry, it is quite an achievement to comprehend, usefully, the mechanics of a camera, even in this day of computer magic. It whirs that sprocket-holed film through a light-proof box and holds it dead still behind the lens, in front of which the shutter just now happens to open to the scene before it, twenty-four times per second. And the very lens itself is a choice between literally dozens. Bewildering? Absolutely, to all but a student of camera optics . . . like your cameraman. The camera and its adjuncts is a maze of photographic possibilities. Proof? Look at the next few pages of illustrations . . . this lens, that lens; this distance from camera to subject; that distance. [See pages 117—119.]

I am not trying to confuse, but only to demand respect for the person who understands and uses all these elements creatively . . . the cameraman.

These three pages of illustrations are the barest sort of survey of lens choices (and their effect on the image) that are available to the cameraman. There's also the "zoom" lens, an adjustable lens mechanism that can be moved (during the shot, if desirable) from, say, 20 mm. to 200 mm. The zoom lens is slightly slower than a fixed-focus lens of the same length, and, therefore, the cameraman has to light a bit brighter; still there are highly skilled and esteemed

Four basic lenses at different distance from the subject.

Here is your basic medium closeup . . .

with a 24mm lens from three feet away . . .

or a 50mm lens from six feet away . . .

or a 135mm lens from ten feet away . . .

or a 200mm lens from fifteen feet away. The cameraman's choice here depends on how much he wants the background to contribute—is there information back there that must be seen?—is the little girl going to turn and walk to the end of the pool?

In short, by changing the distances from camera to subject, one retains the same framing (field of view) but with changing perspectives of the background. With the same distance from camera to subject, the field of view changes. Here's a 28mm lens from ten feet. Notice the background information is quite clear and useful.

A 50mm lens from the same ten feet. The background contains less information.

A 135mm lens from ten feet. Field of view has changed again . . . and the background information is compressed.

A 250mm lens from ten feet and you are closer than you were with the 24mm lens from three feet away, but the background is completely gone.

Photos of Juliet Glennon taken by Jim Glennon.

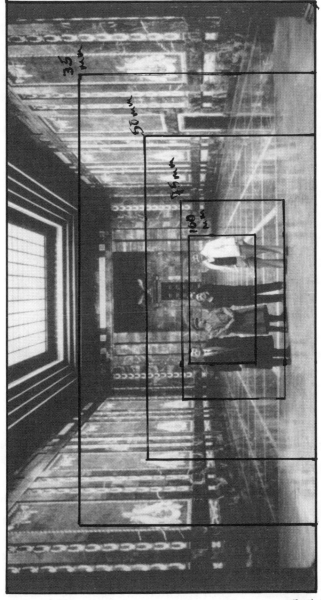

25 mm

35 mm

50 mm

75 mm

100 mm

Various lenses, as marked, all taken with the camera forty-five away.

cameramen who use the zoom almost exclusively. It's a creative choice that must not dismay the producer; indeed, some pictures, for purely artistic, creative reasons, are shot with just one focal-length lens: Bert Glennon, wanting to make the movie *Our Town* seem very real, shot it entirely with a 40 mm.—the lens that comes the closest to the perspective of the human eye.

And the complications do not end there. There are several good types of cameras; knowing the insides of one does not put the camera decision behind one. Some purposes are best served by the Panavision camera . . . some by the Arriflex. And there are others, with different insides.

Knowing the "box," part by part, the cameraman then has a choice of film stocks to ponder: what is their unique usefulness to what he has in mind? High-contrast, low-contrast, fast, slow? Low-light conditions, but a little grainy? High-speed or low-speed? All of 'em useful, from occasion to occasion.

Then, he has to light the scene . . . on location with reflectors and scrims (black cloth light-blockers) plus heavy booster lights . . . in the studio with various qualities and types of electric lights, which may be either arcs or bulbs. Soft light, hard light? Bright, dim?

A cameraman has gone through a long apprenticeship just to get a good hold on these mechanics . . . from assistant, to loader, to operator, to director of photography.

In my experience, there are three types of cameramen for the producer to scratch his head about as he and the director make a choice. Often, the director will have a preference made on the basis of former experience, and, therefore, will find comfort with a familiar man and his way of doing things. If that man is right by the following standards, get him; if he's "off," talk the director into changing his mind.

1. There is the cameraman who has not progressed past being a good mechanic: he knows the machine, film, and lights. Often, the production needs just this type: straight-for-ward, unaffected, clear visibility, day and night easily distinguished, plain as a newspaper photo. Certain documentary type films benefit by this. It simulates bald-eyed reality.

2. There is the cameraman who, through the years, has developed a style that is his stock-in-trade, his raison d'etre. It may be dark and moody, it may be stark contrast (think of *Citizen Kane*), it may always be flame-colored (think of *The Godfather*). Whatever. If you want that speciality, get him. If you don't, be wary; you may get it anyway, either because he assumes that that is what you want or he has forgotten how to do otherwise. He may have lost adaptability.

3. There is the cameraman who can work in many moods at a high level of artistry. Like the fine violinist who can play country-western, rock, Dixieland, Mozart, and the lugubrious waltz. If this man understands the intent of your script, get him.

Often, you and the director will pick a cameraman from having seen work of his that is right on your mark. "We want what you did on *The Deluge*." Often, you both will enter into a tentative agreement with a cameraman, holding off permanence until you have seen eye-to-eye on the "look" that is wanted. (Of course, there are some camera-men of reputation or pride or both who will not take anything less than a pay-or-play commitment; "Why throw dice?" would be my reaction to this challenge).

There are several ways in which a wise producer can help the cameraman do his job. Bring him in early in the preparation process; expensive, perhaps, but not nearly as expensive as something coming up on one of those costly shooting days that the cameraman hadn't been made aware of. Let him see, and comment on, the preliminary set sketches, the wardrobe selections, the prop choices, the locations selected, the second unit plans, if any (to integrate the work of the second unit cameraman with his own first unit work). He will be helpful to you and the director and the artisan involved in choices because he can comment accurately on "photographability." True, he can put, accurately, anything on film, just as the eye sees it; but if you are expecting him to stylize the overall look, check with him before you okay a mauve dinner gown on a brunette actress who is supposed to portray self-conscious good taste. In his pre-planned lighting style, it may have the opposite effect.

On location, he may advise against using a certain building facade for a major scene because, facing north as it does, it will have flat, sunless shadow on it most of the day . . . a dull background for an interesting time in the picture.

Forewarned, your cameraman will bring special equipment to meet special conditions. I am reminded of the storm sequence in *Ryan's Daughter* for which Frederick A. Young, the Academy Award-winning cameraman, brought along a magic device to keep the lens clear in heavy rain: a thin plate of glass about ten inches in diameter was mounted at its center to a high speed motor and this version of an electric fan was attached to the camera where it whirled the glass at very high speed in front of the lens, thus throwing off rain water so fast and so thoroughly that the image was constantly clear.

Arrange with the production manager that the cameraman gets his choice of electrical and grip crew; these men are very important to him in terms of speedily getting what he wants on the set. His camera staff generally goes with him wherever he goes . . . although once in a while an operator is coveted by more than one cameraman.

There soon comes a camera decision that calls for management input as well as artistic input: what aspect ratio of screen height to screen width is to be used in release . . . and, therefore, dictate the cameraman's framing standards? Since it is a marketing tool as well as an artistic tool, management is interested. To list the options: there's the old Academy aperture screen proportion of 1:33 to 1, which TV broadcasts; there is 1:66 to 1, which was used theatrically in the U.S. up to about 1960, but is now "wide-screen" in most European theaters; there is 1:85 to 1 composition, which is what one sees most today; then there's Panavision/ Cinemascope at 2:35 to 1, shot with an anamorphic lens that "squeezes" the image onto 35 mm. film and is "unsqueezed" by the theater projectionist; finally, there is a limited market for 70 mm. prints (now mostly shot on 35 mm. film with an anamorphic lens), a very wide screen with a proportion of 2:21 to 1. (True 65 mm. negative, and the camera to use it, is generally considered to be disproportionately expensive.) The point gained in 70 mm. prints for the projector, made from 65 mm. negative for the camera, is the accessibility of that 5 mm. space for a six-track sound delivery, which is very impressive in behalf of the picture that needs it: space operas, futurism, weak sisters that need bombast and scope to shore them up.

The publicity and advertising departments like the attention-getting strength of Cinemascope and 70 mm. (you will have noticed in your newspapers the heraldry that attends such pictures). And management thinks to itself: "Will this picture sell well without bragging about the size of the screen nor the breadth of the sound? How many theaters do we own or do business with who have 70 mm. equipment and elaborate speaker systems?"

Finally comes the artistic considerations that the producer, the director, and (best judge) the cameraman weigh together. So that you may nod intelligently when the words "Cinemascope" or "one-eight-five-to-one" and "Academy Aperture" or "pan-and-scan the frame" come up, here are some illustrations of what the cameraman is considering. [See pages 125-127.]

The producer should speak right up if a variance from the commonly used 1:85 to 1 ratio is in the wind, from management or distribution, *unless* there's a good reason for going to the larger format. In the case of huge-vista, action-adventure pictures, the wide formats lend a sense of wide-eye excitement for the audience—splendor—and, in most cases, simplistic storytelling. But, in most cases, the large formats merely draw attention to themselves; the audiences notice the wide expanse and, in my opinion, are thus distracted from the screen story. I am very much against anything that distracts an audience from a story-character mode of attention—loud music, cute camera tricks, etc.

Unfortunately for the cameraman, only *some* of the audience will see the picture in the way that *he* framed it in the camera. In the picture's first runs, it, of course, will be as ordered. But, in smaller theaters, less-well-equipped theaters, on television, on airplanes, on VCRs, outside the U.S., it will be shown differently. Especially Cinemascope or 70 mm., but even the more common 1:85 to 1, will be cropped differently; for television, the very wide-screen pictures will be "panned and scanned" in the laboratory. (A process whereby a duplicate negative is made with a lab man laboriously selecting where on that big picture is the most desirable place for a 3:4 image to be. The 70 mm. film holds

Here you see four different aspect ratios, all from the same distance: camera to subject . . . forty-five feet. The first two show a 25mm lens at work, then a 50mm and a 60mm . . . anything longer and one would overshoot the set.

1:33 to 1. Television—Academy Aperture.

1:85 to 1. Most theatrical movies.

2:35 to 1. Panavision.

2:21 to 1. 70mm print proportions.

The original scene

In this case, the cameraman has changed the distances from camera to subject in order to maintain the same composition.

2:35 to 1

1:85 to 1

 ⟨⟨ ⟩⟩

Pan and Scan for television

1:33 to 1 (as seen on television)

2:21 to 1 on 70mm film

man and woman, placed well to the left and well to the right respectively, arguing, and the technician has to pan back and forth or cut from one performer to the other.)

The producer's choice of cameraman for shooting a television movie should follow the above-stated guidelines . . . with the added thought that a present-day methodology (which may well have been corrected by the time you read this) gives a cameraman a problem that the producer must be sensitive to. And that is the practice of editing a television show, be it long or short, on tape. The exposed film negative is developed and a rough, one-light tape of it is then made for the cutter to work with. Result: no "dailies" by which the cameraman can check on the quality of his work and the quality of the film laboratory's work. As a result, he tends to be more careful . . . i.e., take more time on the set, which is expensive. Solve this somehow. Spending the money to provide a positive print of one set-up in each set would be one way to keep this important man comfortable and faster.

But there is an added difficulty for the cameraman in this present-day way of doing things in television: the composite tape that comes out of the dubbing room is "color corrected" by a tape specialist who knows nothing about the peculiarities of the film on which it was shot (a process much like translating an English novel into Russian with only a Russian-English dictionary in hand . . . it won't read right!) Result: your hard working cameraman sees the broadcast and is appalled at the difference between what he intended and what the public is seeing. The producer in television must be aware of this gap in quality control and defeat it if he can.

In features, make sure that the cameraman even participates in the final positive-print color-correction process at the lab; he'll do it at night if he has to. All the thought and planning and effort that this book goes on about comes to a final and permanent rest in this artist's little black box. Choose carefully!

A producer, quite properly, stands in some awe at the complicated and inter-locking elements at the cameraman's disposal. Recall the admittedly sketchy details in this chapter, if you will. Starting at the outset of shooting, there's a choice of screen proportions (even that is not entirely firm, for space has to be allowed for adaptation of that image to other screens and other mediums); a choice of camera (but that is not firm either, for it may be wise to change camera types occasionally to meet certain shooting conditions or needs); a choice of film stock which may vary from set to set; a choice of lighting techniques (shot by shot); a choice of lenses. And there are other choices, too complicated for you or I to know: like "over-crank" or "under-crank" the camera, resulting in a slower-moving image or faster-moving image, respectively.

Choose carefully!

10

GRIP, SET OPERATIONS, AND ELECTRICAL

These men are all under the direction of the cameraman; he should select them, or, at least, be empowered to change personnel here if he is dissatisfied with the men whom the studio or the production manager supply.

A grip is basically a highly skilled carpenter; he can lay dolly track, put up a platform for a heavy arc light, rig a holding iron so that a porch swing doesn't stir during closeups; you name it. He, too, has a box full of wonders that he has picked up during his career, and is often challenged by some joker about the availability of a sky-hook or a two-handed dormer-gear (?). There are generally four to ten men in his crew, depending on the complexity of the day's work. Often, on location, where complex improvisation is demanded, he may have more . . . a painter, a greensman, a special crane-operator . . . all falling under the catch-all name of "set operations."

The electricians' title explains them; from the power source on the stage or from the generator on location, they run the power lines to the lights . . . set them in place at the direction of the head electrician, called a "gaffer," who has been told by the cameraman where he wants what lighting effect. Once again, that gaffer should be the cameraman's selection. The producer should begin stalking around through the chain of command if it is found out that the cameraman is not content with his grip, set operations, or electrical crew.

These elements of production, both equipment and manpower, should come together routinely under the mandate of the production manager.

11
PRODUCTION SOUND

This on-the-set work is called "production sound" to properly separate it from the "post-production sound" function, which I will get to in Chapter Twenty-three. The responsibility of production sound is to get as clean (uncluttered) a dialogue track as possible with the proper distance perspective. There is a mixer on the set, operating the sound recorder, which is adjusted to a flat response so that any equalization needed can be done in the re-recording process later; and there is a boom operator on the set who generally works from a mobile platform, moving a directional microphone from actor's lips to actor's lips, just out of the camer's top-frame. Sometimes circumstances force the use of a concealed body-mike (for instance, the performer is at some distance from the camera and a closeup is not planned), but sound quality suffers and this take usually becomes a "cue track" for the dialogue-replacement process later.

I can tell from the number of pictures I see that I cannot hear, or, should I say, cannot understand, that there are some producers who do not pick their sound crew carefully, or do not help them do their job, which is *to provide a clean dialogue track that does not require post-production dub-*

bing to be comprehensible. It often happens that the mixer is ignored or waved off when, after a take, he declares his dissatisfaction: "Once more, please." What a nuisance, when everything else went so well! The mixer heard a long, high squeak from the dolly movement . . . an airplane passed over the stage . . . an actress surprisingly turned her head away from the mike before the boom operator could adjust the rehearsed moves . . . the leading man slipped into his natural accent (he's Italian and took English elocution lessons), etc. Unless the producer plans to spend a good deal of money dubbing the dialogue later (actor for a day's pay, a sound crew, a stage, etc.), he'd best give the mixer the same privileges that the director and the cameraman enjoy: "Once more, please." (Besides, dubbing is not always satisfactory . . . the perspective can go wrong, lips will not be in sync, the take will sometimes have a different resonance than the dialogue that precedes or follows, etc.)

With that privilege of commanding another take must go a commensurate talent; it's a tough job, sitting there with earphones on head, dials in hand, apprehensive about the defective stage door that lets street sounds in despite a baffle being erected around it, or the arc light that characteristically spits once in a while (if it spits between words, it can be cut out manually). Also, players will fall into habits that they have been trained to control . . . lisping, speaking too fast, slurring . . . and the mixer will detect them and, rightly, call for remedy.

So pick carefully, Producer, considering the sound problems you can foresee: the star is notorious for sloppy articulation; the leading woman gets shrill (manageable by dial if the mixer knows it's coming); one of the supporting players has a barely controllable lisp. In view of the howls that set up when the mixer wants another take, hire a strong mind who insists on prevailing.

Recording on location is sometimes a different matter; it can be so unpreventably noisy that all the sound man can hope for is a comprehensible cue track to guide the performers in the post-production dubbing room.

The producer should have a chat with the sound mixer on the location set about "wild tracking" dialogue scenes where there was uncontrollable noise; after the noise has abated (perhaps a train went noisily by right in the middle of a very difficult performance) or later in that same day (having moved to quieter circumstances), get the same group of actors to stand before the set microphone and play the scene wild (no camera). With any luck, they will remember the pace, the intonations, the passions of the scene; I've seen many a wild track, thus obtained, fall right into place in the editor's room.

Also, have the location sound mixer silence the crew for a moment and take an "ambiance" track of a minute or so on each location; it helps the dubbing mixers balance location dialogue and effects with later wild and completely silent sound when they put it all together in the dubbing process.

In continental European production, the sound man usually only concerns himself with a cue track because the picture is often being made with performers of several nationalities and languages; it all has to be dubbed, one for each country of release.

Producer! You've spent a lot of time on the script dialogue; make sure that it can be heard.

12
SPECIAL EFFECTS

This miracle worker generally has a look of surprised indignation on his face. "You want what?" The bedsheets are tumbling about as if someone were climbing out of bed . . . they're moving around . . . but there's no one in the bed? The star lifts up this cement park bench and throws it in the lake? The slot machine walks up to the dice table and rolls a seven? Such stuff.

Ingenuity being his stock in trade, the special-effects man always manages it somehow. I remember a "Twilight Zone" episode that called for the star (having suddenly been awarded tremendous strength) to be awakened by an alarm clock on his bedside table for which he reaches to quiet its bell and crushes it to the table surface with this gentle gesture. Our special-effects man, Virgil Beck, said, "What?" Then he built an alarm clock of thin lead, capped it with a similarly colored steel disc to which a string was attached; the string ran down through the clock and through the table to a pulley nailed to the stage floor and thence to Beck's hand off-screen. At the cry of "Action!", the star wakened, stretched toward the clock, put a languid, sleepy hand on its alarm button and gave a gentle push downward; Beck pulled on the string and down went the clock at the pace set by the actor.

Their "commonplace" are explosions and the results thereof, and gunfire and its residue. You've seen such time and again, but it takes a real craftsman to rig these events so that no one is hurt and the effects look real. Most are controlled by remote electrical signals, either a wired or a wireless signal setting off the charge. They manage all wind and rain effects, going fireplaces, lightning. So the producer doesn't need to be involved in sci-fi to need a good special-effects man. He's part of the standard crew, for no one knows when the need will arise . . . for instance, the director decides that it would be more interesting if the star's reading-light bulb exploded, causing the darkness in which the hold-up man makes his move, rather than having him merely sitting there in the dark.

Off stage, and often far from the standard studio, are the special-effects companies who create special effects on a giant scale: a space shuttle rescue, a 747 crashes into one of the Egyptian pyramids, Stallone scales Mt. Everest hand-over-hand, the Empire State Building crumbles into rubble, a burning asteroid approaches Earth. These artisans combine miniature skills, frame-by-frame exposure cameras, animation techniques, background and foreground projection screens, even mirrors, to accomplish almost anything a writer can think up. They provide the background film by which Superman flies through New York city. They provide the raw material by which the optical printer combines a sword fight between two actors (shot weeks ago) and the futuristic tower (a miniature), aswarm with bats (animated), on top of which they seem to be fighting.

The special-effects man on the set must be carefully picked, but his work is mostly ingenuity, not expense. But the big, off-the-set effects, chosen for their uniqueness in the audience's experience are, of necessity, very expensive: "No one has done that before." Even if the desired effect calls for techniques used before, they have to be re-rigged, repainted, etc.

Faced with the question: "How can this be done and can I afford it?" the producer would be well advised to shop about a bit for estimates on the job *and* for planned suggestions on how to achieve the effect. There are several ways to accomplish some effects, and what you are shopping for is inventiveness as well as cost effectiveness. These companies are in business and, within reason, will go to some expense to demonstrate how and what they intend to put on the screen, and at what cost.

So do not despair; the writer has called for a visual phenomenon that you can't imagine as do-able. Give the problem to one of the special-effects folks and they'll amaze you; not only is it their job to amaze you, it's their pleasure. It may take a while, but I've yet to hear of a producer being told, "It can't be done!" [See pages 138-141 for three examples of a producer's dilemma being worked out by a special-effects procedure.]

Inside The Third Reich dramatized the days and the work of Albert Speer, Hitler's architect. E. Jack Neuman needed to show action in at least one room of the Reich Chancellory which Spear had designed. All that remained of the World War-destroyed Chancellory interior were a few snapshots. Such a set would be far too expensive to build.

The specialists at Introvision used this real snapshot of the main Chancellory meeting room...split it into two perfectly matching matte images, one of which was projected behind this actor ...

Photos: © Introvision Studios, Inc.

... walking on the stage riser with painted lines indicating where he was to walk ... the other matte was projected onto a glass between actor and camera ... note the sawhorse indicating tabletop height in the snapshot...with this result: The actor walked into the room from the left, walked around the table, put his hand on its top (sawhorse) and departed screen right.

In short, when a producer faces a set cost that he can't afford, maybe he can take a picture of what he needs and Introvision can do the rest.

Note: there is a quality plus to this method. The above shot was made with a single pass of the camera, rather than having to composite the two mattes and the actor onto a second place of negative.

For his film *Stand By Me,* Rob Reiner wanted some real excitement for his runaway kids—how about having them caught on a railroad bridge? He took his wish to Introvision, who photographed a fast train approaching and crossing a bridge.

Then, in the Introvision studio, they put the two young actors on a high platform, had them crawl in a panicky way, and projected the approaching train (film above) through their patented reflective process.

And here's the result. The kids jumped onto the near platform in the nick of time. Photos: © Introvision Studios, Inc.

If you remember *Driving Miss Daisy,* this is the house in which she lived. The only problem with it for the producer was that it had to be seen in the movie during the snowy winter, too; you can't extend the shooting schedule to include two seasons, so . . .

you have a good special effects company do Miss Daisy's house as a minature. Photos: © Introvision Studios, Inc.

13
WARDROBE

The clothes that the performers wear, and *how* they wear them, are their chief weapons in characterization. Wardrobe is also the performers' chief source of comfort about their task—to characterize someone! It helps to look the part, going in! [See page 143, Michelle Pfeiffer.]

No amount of emphasis here will overdo the importance of the producer's responsibility toward the picture and performers in this department. Early on, and best with the director by your side by now, you will work with the woman costumer or the man costumer or both, in deciding whether the wardrobe task can be adequately solved by selecting from standard items: the players own wardrobe (carefully picked over, for some have no inkling about what suits them best) . . . or selecting out of a studio/public costume house . . . or shopping at the department stores.

Naturally, it's more than just a matter of good taste in clothes; flamboyant character, flamboyant clothes; a messpot, messy clothes. But colors also enter into it; and here the art director's work and the cameraman's eye can help all hands (I've mentioned the virtue in having the cameraman on hand early). A severe black business-cut suit for the leading actress is not going to be seen well enough to make a

Here are examples of how a wardrobe designer helped a fine actress into a tough characterization and also helped the story progression. Michelle Pfeiffer, in *The Fabulous Baker Boys*, not only had to play a tartish broad, but also convey an underlying potential for sweetness that gave a chance, scene by scene, for a love story to work out to the audience's satisfaction. How do you do "tart" which is sexy and appealing, without also doing "cheap" which is a turn-off for a love object. Well, look. Lisa Jensen, Costume Designer, and Ms. Pfeiffer brought it off!

statement in a dining room that is planned for an overall black look (for some other dramatic reason); it's better to go for a patterned dress, or just a medium blue suit. Then some materials look good in motion (it's for a dance scene) and others do not. As in set design and decoration and props, a period picture throws the wardrobe designer into a different and very confining area; authenticity must be observed whereas modern wardrobe is infinite in its choices.

You and the director might well decide, in order to do justice to the role or to a name player, that standard, off-the-rack clothes just won't do; budget extravagantly for a fine costume designer and a custom-made wardrobe. And give this designer time for research and design preliminaries; it will pay. Even in a "today" picture, there's research; you can bet that Marilyn Vance-Straker, the costume designer on *Pretty Woman*, had to drive up and down Hollywood Boulevard a couple of nights to find out what hookers are wearing this season.

Or, say the story goes back to 1960 before leaping ahead to 1991: How did they dress then? Well, first off, the costume designer goes by the provable premise that most people remember the look of the 1960s by the movies they saw then. How did Shirley Maclaine dress in *The Apartment*? How did Laurence Harvey dress in *Butterfield 8*? The careful costume designer will also research the materials of the time. Then, in case the story involves aging or a peculiar appearance, a meeting with makeup and hairdress is necessary so that all hands are playing the same tune.

It is very important that the cast all feel that they are being considerately dealt with on this picture (it's ego-massage to be sure) . . . that they and their appearance are important. *This feeling will improve their performance.* Have wardrobe sketches made . . . attend fittings . . . show that pains have been taken . . . then, sure that the best possible design work has been done, turn to the ego-management phase of your work with an enthusiastic comment on the results.

The maintenance and immediate availability of the these clothes . . . every externally visible garment . . . is in the hands of the man costumer and the woman costumer on the set. They see to it that they are kept clean, ready to be changed for what the performer is wearing at the moment . . . new scene, five minutes to change! All cataloged and numbered in their script so that exactly the same threads will be worn in Scene 1, shot the first day, and Scene 2, shot on the twelfth day; the script clerk will have confirming notes, but don't count on the performer to remember.

What the producer is looking for here, when he confirms the production manager's choice, is meticulousness, creativity, and, oh yes, tact (the leading actress *does* have figure problems, requiring special draping efforts).

14
MAKEUP AND HAIRDRESS

Okay, so there's another factor in the performer's self-confidence as he/she strides onto the set. Their heads.

Both makeup and hairdress can also play a part in helping a player toward a successful characterization. Flamboyant: heavy makeup and hi-style hairdo. Messpot: no makeup and overdue at the barber's. And those in-between.

The design of each, especially for the women, is a high art. The big studios in former times, with valuable actresses under contract, had full-time, highly paid artists whose sole job it was to make those actresses' hair and faces look just right. These designers set the styles in makeup and hairdress for millions of women by the examples of their work seen on the screen. The need for the same sort of attention is noticeable today in the picture credits that name the leading actress' makeup and hairdress experts.

Of course, sometimes the story demands that these two artists de-glamorize the lady . . . make the beautiful into the dowdy and plain . . . so that there's somewhere to go when she inherits her uncle's millions and visits a beauty shop for the first time. [See Sally Field on page 147.]

Adequate time for research comes into play here, too. Hairdos of the '60s? Hooker's hairdos? Newest makeup

Here is Sally Field, as seen in *Places in the Heart.* A perfect example of makeup and hairdress (wardrobe too) helping a fine actress perform contary to her real appearance.

Photo: Courtesy Tri-Star Pictures, Inc. Wardrobe Designer, Ann Roth. Makeup by Bob Mills. Hairdress by Paul Le Blanc.

fashions (purple lipstick)? And what is Wayne Finkelman, costume designer on Fox's *For The Boys*, turning up historically in order to age Bette Midler through the '60s and '70s?

The performers' ebullience that comes with a bit of thoughtful attention here is the reward that comes to the producer who participates mindfully in the makeup/hair design process. And it pays, to insure the full returns on his investment in careful casting, to have very talented people attending to that head.

A major role in the visual success of "The Twilight Zone" was played by William Tuttle, head of the makeup and hairdress department at MGM, and his staff. Whenever I needed something above and beyond the high-level routine available from Tuttle's appointee on the set, I turned to him and got the special-effects man's standard reply: "What?" Make Dean Stockwell look Japanese? Put a third eye in the middle of this actor's forehead? This character is an alien from another planet (we were always doing that)? Design a race of people (we need four of 'em) who are *repulsively* ugly? Well, Tuttle and his crew did them all, and to our directors' great satisfaction. And enjoyed doing them.

In more conventional fare than" Twilight Zone," a producer will find himself needing a William Tuttle, just the same. For instance, aging a player is very difficult to do well. So is beautifying a plain face. Or uglifying a beautiful face. (In both aging and uglifying, so called appliances are used: bits of metal or cloth or cottonball, glued to the face and thus changing its contours). There's the problem, occasionally, of disguising, for a moment, a well-known face. In picking and fitting hair pieces . . . for both men and women.

It's worth reiterating: Producer, remember to find and use the best talents available . . . they can make your picture better . . . a practice made feasible by knowing what they are capable of doing when asked. [See pages 149-152 of Meg Ryan, Ken Branagh, and Emma Thompson.]

I can only guess what went through the minds of Steven Spielberg, Kathleen Kennedy, and Frank Marshall (the Amblin production team) when they had the final script of *Joe Versus the Volcano* on their desks. But it was not an extraordinary dilemma: there was a strong man's role, and then three fragmentary, however strong, women's roles that were not big enough to attract a star actress to any one of them; they wanted more "name value" than just the leading man. So, admiring Meg Ryan's talents, they thought that maybe she could play all three parts . . . with a little help from hairdress and makeup. Results: Can do! [See next page.]

Many in the audience did not catch on and they were not provided with a clue from the up-front credits; Ms. Ryan's name was only in the end credits. (Her name was up front in the ads!)

Photos: Courtesy of Amblin—Warner Bros. Makeup by Leonard Engleman. Hairdress by Barbara Lorenz.

Ken Branagh, as both star and director of *Dead Again*, and his wife, Emma Thompson, faced the task of portraying two people in 1950 and their reincarnated sexual opposites in 1991 . . . a formidable acting chore. They turned for assistance to their makeup and hairdress experts, Dan Striepeke and Kathy Blondell, with these amazing results:

1950

1950

1991

15
PUBLICITY

It will pay the producer well to give some time to picking the right party here, plus the still photographer/aide. When the distribution people come to selling the picture to the public, you'll be glad that there is pre-release material and during-release material, both copy and pictures, that was skillfully gathered while you were shooting. Naturally, in both, you want experienced judgment skills in what is publishable: What do magazines want? Newspapers? Gossip columnists? Moody essayists on "the cinema"?

Generally, both these experts are outgoing, genial types who can "con" their way into the hearts of players . . . thus getting pictures and stories that might otherwise be withheld for reasons of reticence, modesty, or, heaven forbid, sheer dislike of your publicity people's brassy qualities.

16
TRANSPORTATION

Get the right transportation captain and you're home free. Again, a highly skilled man who is worth pressing the production manager for the best. He is in charge of all your wheels; he rents 'em, he dispatches 'em, he keeps track of 'em by radio. And when you go to location, either local or distant, he commands the "pecking order" for parking each truck and car; since most locations are confined as to parking space (even in a western in the middle of desert Arizona, the wheels have to park out of camera sight), it is a major convenience for the captain to have parked every bit of equipment sensibly, in full awareness of their contents and the importance of their nearness to the set or the unimportance of their farness. Here we are, shooting in an antique shop on a commercial street, where the police, in pursuance of our permit, have cleared the parking areas; our wheels' parking is confined to the curbsides adjacent and out of camera range. The captain mistakenly parks the makeup trailer nearest, and the production van with heavy camera and dollies aboard a full block away. Chaos!

There's a good story from my experience about a transportation captain of dynamic habits . . . brisk, he was; shooting completed, late one afternoon, he sent this truck into town, that bus, that car, that one, that ??? . . . looking about for the last vehicle, he found himself alone and wheelless on a location five hard miles from our motel.

17
LOCATION

Looking for location sites is basically an act of great optimism: you're hoping that someone had the foresight and kindness to build a house, a street, a factory that exactly suits your storytelling needs. In the studio, you build to suit your story; on location, you suit your story to what has been built. So, you keep looking, hoping to find the City Hall you would have built if you had the money.

The first problem that arises after management or money says, "let's go!" is figuring out when to start shooting . . . six weeks . . . twelve weeks from that exhilarating and affirmative moment? If the locations are difficult or numerous, the producer should wangle plenty of preparation time. Other factors can have a bearing on the start date . . . like a pay-or-play start commitment with a star, promised delivery date if it's a movie-for-TV, construction time for a difficult set . . . but the time it takes to find the right locations is, perforce, indefinite, and you don't want to settle for an inadequate location because of starting-date pressures.

The production manager will have selected a specialist in locations . . . the location manager . . . who has extensive picture files of all the locations he and his friends have ever been on . . . and who, preliminarily, will have looked over some likely spots ahead of time.

Besides the production manager and location manager, you should have the director and the cameraman with you on any location scout. This is not a luxury, it's an economy because, in so doing, you are compelled to face up to likely expenses before you spend the money. You find a great, small-town street; it may not occur to you, but it will to the cameraman, that it faces south, running east and west, which means that it will have sun on it all day. This may be fine for a short scene, but there are trees and lampposts whose shadows will be falling at different slants across the storefronts every minute, making it difficult to match shots during the whole ten hours that is necessary to shoot a long scene. Slow and, therefore, expensive! The north-facing side of a street, if it can be found and is suitable, will be okay for the long scene, but, shaded all day, it will need some detail . . . trees, lampposts, and a hot arc light here and there. A street running north and south will have a half day's shade, a half-day's sun, each side. Or, the trucks cannot drive sensibly near to this location; hand carry equipment for a half mile? Thus, you foresee trouble, which is the best way of staying out of it.

A lot depends on whether you are looking for modern locations, ten years ago, or Biblical times. For the latter, you will build sets in the right sort of terrain, out of sight of other buildings. Period locations can often be found, even in big cities; there is a several-square-block area just off the Hollywood freeway as it approaches downtown Los Angeles that, barring television aerials (you pay householders to take them down for a day or two), is a perfect 1920 mid-west, small-town, residential area.

The best starting point for a location scout is to consider the actual location called for in the script: New England fishing village, Grand Canyon boating, New York ghetto, a

Miami beach, the shoulders of Mt. Everest? Some real locations are out of the question as too dangerous or too expensive . . . then you start looking for substitutes and for ways of restricting the scope of the shooting so that a deception will go unnoticed. Also, when you get right down to it, some locations are not as handsome in reality as they are in people's minds . . . you have to upgrade them somewhere else. Or, having studied the real, and far distant locale, turn to the location manager who is leading this search and ask for a visual substitute nearby.

Once a location is found, the location manager will arrange location matters well ahead of your arrival, matters that are essential for the shoot to work smoothly. He will have gotten acquainted with the city government (no matter what size the city is), making clear to them how much money the shooting company is bringing into the local economy—hotels, meals, local car and truck rentals, local hiring, etc. Many favors come from this money flow. He presses for (and gets) police department cooperation in the necessary street traffic tie-ups, which sometimes calls for re-routing or hours of complete blockage. The Chamber of Commerce will help; the local employment offices will help to find carpenters, electricians, extras, etc., all at the location manager's push. He will also have completed rental arrangements for the chosen shooting sites . . . homes, offices, buildings, etc. If the location schedule is a long one, he will find a vacant warehouse or school auditorium to rent in which to build a cover set or two. He will drive a hard bargain for the crew's hotel arrangements—what management won't cut a deal to have fifty or more rooms go in block for a week, two weeks, a month? In short, he is in charge of making St. Louis or Chicago or Cross Creek work smoothly and cost effectively.

The location manager's workload varies, for some pictures

plan out best by being made entirely on location, using real offices, apartments, and cover sets for a rainy day. And some need very few locations and are shot mainly in the studio. Now those last two sentences seem to cover simple ground, simply. Yet it takes complex planning . . . then alternate planning . . . to discover which sentence makes the most sense for this particular picture. It's often dollars vs. looks, for locations are expensive: you transport most of the crew there, you house them, feed them, move them about in trucks, busses and cars! Maybe you can fake it less expensively in the studio. *Au contraire*, some stories demand a location that cannot be reproduced reasonably or sensibly and the expenses of taking a crew to location is a bargain.

The director should be along on any scout, if only to have that location in his mind as he thinks out his preparation for the scenes that he must shoot there. Or he may have a concept for a location look that enhances the story; and he looks and looks and looks. Producer, be patient with this.

As you can sense, location demands and the consequent decisions can be thornier than a cactus stand. Plans for location requirements change as the location search progresses from area to area; this locale is fine for scenes 22 through 37 . . . and this locale is fine for scenes 78 through 91 . . . but each is only two pages long and the two sites are seven miles apart. Hey, here's luck; two locales that will do nicely, only a block apart!

Give the location-scout process ample time; five men . . . producer, director, cameraman, production manager, and location manager . . . traveling about is money well spent in view of the economies, as well as the dramatic pertinence, of the right spot.

Because of the riches of the MGM backlot, "The Twilight Zone" only had to go on distant locations for Ext. Asteroid, a desert (once or twice), a baseball diamond, a railroad crossing . . . that's all. But on High Chaparral, a western, I was constantly in and out of Tucson hotel rooms because we shot the interiors on show #1 at the studio, then the exteriors for show #1 on location, then the exteriors on show #2 on location; then back to the studio for the interiors on show #2 . . . interiors on show #3 . . . etc.

Having found the right locations, the work has just begun for the production manager and the location manager. They are basically shaping-up a studio in a movie-wise desolate spot; no lights in town, no cameras, no props, no wardrobe houses, no grip equipment . . . nothing cinematic. Bring it! There may be highly skilled carpenters in town, but what do they know about the fakery of paper walls or stairways going nowhere; then there are light scaffolds, high camera platforms, dolly tracks . . . built in twenty minutes, please.

We've spoken of housing the crew, but there's also the matter of feeding them on the set at midday, as well as being assured that, with expense money, they will find good eating publicly.

Projection facilities must be set up so that dailies can be seen. And that can't be at a local theater, for dailies are seen in the evening after work. Complicated shipping arrangements must be made for today's negative film to go to the lab for development and printing and for the positive film of yesterday's work to come back from the lab each day for viewing.

There's an added burden on the production manager and the location manager (and everybody else) when you go to a desolate location: an idyllic South Sea isle . . . the Philippine jungle. A tent city has to be built which meets the company's living and recreational needs for weeks, sometimes months. Think twice about choosing such a location (Are you sure there's no other way to do it?). It's a hard strain on everyone's capacity to perform well.

In many places in the world now there are government supported bureaus whose job it is to entice motion picture companies to come there, and, having succeeded, use a lot of their civic muscle to help you get what you need, be it hotel accommodations, a caterer, etc. Reason: a movie company brings a lot of money into a local economy.

Some locations are a pleasure, almost touristy . . . Seattle for three weeks, shooting at the University of Washington; good restaurants, wonderful people around one, trips across Puget Sound on Sunday. Hawaii in the fall. Munich in the winter. But then there's Death Valley in summer with temperatures up to 135 degrees, some crew members insisting on a nice cold Coke and passing out a half hour later, sleepless nights because of no air conditioning in the motel (they weren't used to customers in late June), etc. No fun. But there was no other way to afford a picture that said, "There's this guy who lives on a faraway planet."

There is another virtue of location shooting besides the sheer fun of travel: you learn something about how other people live and think, be they Hawaiians or other Californians; you are in the business of reaching them emotionally, and the better you know their daily lives and concerns the better for you.

18
STUDIO AND EQUIPMENT RENTALS

This won't take long. If you are shooting with a studio affiliation, the stage space and the shooting equipment is part of your overhead charge (a percentage of dollars spent directly). If you are an independent, working out of an office up until shooting time, your production manager will compare prices around town for the best rental deal that suits your needs.

If renting, one studio can suit your needs better than another. This one has a small-town street on the backlot; this one has a theater auditorium on a stage (from a former picture, left standing); this one is hungry for business and prices out lower.

Despite the routine sound of this, it is a big item on any budget and the producer should keep on top of the choices made and the prices paid.

19
FILM, RAW STOCK
AND PROCESSING

This book is about what a producer does . . . and he doesn't do much about the film stock used nor the laboratory in which it is processed and printed. He is wise enough to leave both choices to the cameraman. There are various film stocks available, competitive as to price and level of innovation, company-by-company, and as to what can be accomplished with them. A cameraman will very likely change the stock from scene to scene if the dramatic demands or production difficulties change that much. As I mentioned when covering the cameraman: fast, slow, soft, hard?

Laboratory? A studio may own one or have continuing commitments with one. As an independent, a producer would be wise to use the lab that suits his cameraman best.

20
MISCELLANEOUS

I will stick to my budget format to explain some costs that present themselves, and are beyond the producer's control. He must know of them, for they can shock. Mandatory State Workers' Compensation and Union-contract fringe benefits covering retirement, health funds, and vacation allowances can amount to as much as eighteen percent of your payroll if you are non-union, or as much as thirty-two percent if you are IATSE.

Then there's are insurance costs that can mount up to the $100,000 to $300,000 range, such as: cast and director death or illness coverage, property damage on location, lost negative film, travel accident, crew injury, third-party liability, equipment damage, etc.

If you are in a studio, there is an overhead charge of thirty to forty percent of direct costs that covers many things mentioned elsewhere, like stage space, studio shooting equipment and facilities, but also covers a lot of mundane items like office space and supplies, messenger service, telephone, photocopying, legal necessities, computer services. As an independent, you will have to pay these expenses directly, item by item, to the amount of $100,000 on a small film to millions on a large one. These items of expense are like death and taxes: not much that ingenuity can change.

21
EDITORIAL

Francis Coppola says that one creates a picture three times. First, you write it. Second, you shoot it. Third, you edit it. Each is a creative process which depends on the ingredients you have in hand at the moment. At the picture's inception, you've got words and your imagination; in the middle ground, you've got actors and sets and a camera; at the end, you've got the film . . . rigid in what is on it, flexible in what order you put it together . . . with music and sound effects embellishments coming up.

Or, to put it another way, the writer sets up margins—the "field" for the director to play in; then the director sets up margins—the "field" for the editor to play in. Now you and the director and the editor set up margins—the "field" for the audience to play in.

The editor is a major contributor to the film's final impact. The pacing of the film's emotional moments—the timing in delivering surprises, knowing just when to cut to the scene's punch line—teasing with pauses, hyping up a tense scene with quick jolting cuts. Certainly, the director has been thinking of these very tactics (among others) while shooting, but the editor has done it more often, and learned more lessons the hard way by doing it wrong a few times.

Perhaps, too, he is better than others in visualizing what sound effects and music and screen size are going to add to the bald film going through his tiny, cutting-room viewing machine.

I have found that the best editor for any project is found by type casting. Has this one cut the sort of picture you're making? Does this one's personal tastes run toward sentimentality or violence? And, most important to my way of thinking, does this one have a talent for quick adaptability to new ground rules; by which I mean, the mental capacity to shift quickly to a new approach . . . not necessarily because of a problem arising, but because of a thrilling opportunity opening up. If there is a problem, be it in one scene or the entire picture, the solution often lies in doing a 180 degree turnabout . . . how would the scene work (and do we have the film coverage for it?) if it played off the girl instead of the man? What if, instead of telling the story chronologically, we cut it to go back and forth in time? A fine editor can see those turnarounds in his mind's eye in a moment, and, having seen it thus, can execute it quickly for everyone's consideration. On the other hand, a different sort of mind, who must take step one and two in any enterprise before he even comprehends step three, will be a slow editor and, in fact, not very good because his mind does not leap quickly and thoroughly to new ideas; beware of the ponderous mind . . . it has no place in maintaining vitality in the cutting process, not even if you're making Ibsen.

At this point in the producer's work, the expensive frenzy of production and all its moment-to-moment perils are behind him. The only ones on salary are the editor and an assistant, and they are busy preparing a first assembly of the film (variously called a first rough cut, or the cutter's cut); generally this takes about two and a half to three weeks after shooting has finished. (The editor has been assembling scenes, day-by-day, whenever a given scene was completely covered; but he cannot be completely up-to-date.) He will not have taken out any lines, much less sequences, and will have cut it in script order; he may know full well that this version is not quite right . . . some things didn't work, but he is obliged to put it all together per the script. Naturally, he will have cut the inner scene-coverage together according to his best judgment, while also recalling the reactions he got from the director and the producer during the dailies.

Be patient about the time it takes the editor to put this first cut together. For, in all, he probably has 140,000 feet of film (maybe 250,000 feet) in his cutting room—which he assembles down to, let's say, a fat, free and generous 11,000 feet (ready for tightening to 9,000-10,000 feet). If this footage seems excessive to you, look at the script supervisor's sample on page 88 and you'll see how film accumulates: there is one page, five set-ups and about 500 feet of film for the editor to bring down to about 90 feet.

Now, editor, producer, and director put their hearts in their mouths and run it. It's never perfect; you've got to go through Coppola's third stage: create the movie yet a third time with ingredients shaped a little differently than you had imagined them back at the second Coppola stage. At the end of that first running, if you're in luck, it may take no more than a nod all around for everyone to know what needs doing. It may have gone together very smoothly; just a little fine-tuning to be done. The Coppola third stage comes easily! Or it may have a few disappointing scenes, or it may just not work at all! Then there's a little discouraged, head down talk; but I favor very *little* talk at this stage. It's now in the director's hands for his privileged "director's cut;" plunging into an hour and a half or two of storytelling . . . four hundred to eight hundred cuts . . . with a story sagging in the middle and two bad performances (let's say)!

At this point, the producer shouldn't clutter up the editor's and the director's mind-focus with what may be diversionary ideas. (Incidentally, some directors try to insist that this first rough cut be run for him and the editor alone, without the producer or anyone else, and that he gets the next cut also done in privacy. I am all in favor of this second cut being done by the director and the editor alone, but I insist on seeing this cutters "first assembly." How else am I to know what film is available, unless I remember dailies foot by foot, with which to solve problems that remain after the director's cut?)

The producer must be aware of the bag of tricks available to this process of assembling several hundred camera set-ups, especially if there are repairs to be made. The director will have used some of them as he did his work; then, when he shows the producer his handiwork, together they work with even more of these devices. What tricks? The editor knows of hundreds . . . like blow-ups of a camera angle which may achieve a closeup you didn't have or get rid of an aspect of the full shot that you do not want; there are startlingly quick cuts, languid dissolves. There are tricks for shortening a scene . . . or for taking a certain actor out of the scene altogether. Plan to ask the composer for strong music to punch up a sequence. Count on the sound-effects editor to goose up the noise around a scene; it's lifeless now. There's a long list of such devices at a good editor's disposal.

Then there is the possibility (which is a lot of work) of re-ordering the events . . . the sequential structure . . . of the story. For instance, think back to the last multiple-story picture you saw . . . one that keeps track of various events supposedly going on at the same time; let's say *American Graffiti*, which told of a high school graduation night, as experienced by four different groups of kids. I happen to know that that picture was cut and recut and recut many

times so that you were never too long with group #1, left
group #2 in an exciting situation just as you cut to #3 who,
just as you expected from your last sight of them, are in
serious trouble, not forgetting meanwhile that in group #4,
Sam was about to make out with Mabel. But let's try going
to #4 first, then to #3. It was a juggling act.

Or take a mystery story. It's very delicate country,
telling too much and letting the audience get boringly ahead
of you or not telling enough and having an audience that
will never catch up (nor care to).

I find that inviting a professional stranger into a
screening is a big help; you know the story *too* well. Let him
tell you what he saw, where he was a mite bored, and ask
about the joke he didn't get.

And, sometimes, if you have the luxury of time, you
can let a troublesome film, or just a troublesome sequence,
languish for a week or so . . . see if an idea doesn't come.
And, sometimes, if you've got the money, retakes or added
scenes can be afforded and help.

The producer should also judge whether the cutting
should be done in the new tape techniques that TV has
been using for years. You will need an editor who is not
only experienced in storytelling (which not all TV tape
editors are) but knows the mechanics of a tape editing
machine. It is faster because of the computerized way that it
stores the separate cuts . . . at your fingertips. You can try a
different sequence of cuts in a given scene in a split second
. . ."Want to try the girl's closeup there?" Boom, there it is.
Doesn't work! Back the way it was before. This equipment
is expensive to rent, much less buy, but it's a sure way to
gain time if you are in a hurry for the finished product. The
machines on which to practice the art of editing a picture
are in a constant state of transition and development; at the

moment, more than half of the features being worked on are in Moviolas, or, perhaps, Kem tables; most all TV editing is now on tape machines of various kinds. It really matters not what equipment is used . . . it's the creative thinking that goes into it that counts.

One day, the film will look its best and you'll show it to management, your money people, your exhibitor friend. There'll be comments, criticism, maybe even an improving idea. Or they will drive you back to the cutting room with coarse language. Y'see, in that private world of the cutting room, all hands can delude themselves that this hurdle was cleared, that this scene is not really too long and too dull; you absolutely MUST have this scene in for clarity . . . come to find out, matters are completely clear without it. It's back to the drawing boards.

Then, in further pursuit of the Coppola editing-is-creation-too theory, you will try to learn from a sneak preview or two, using temporary music and the crude work print, right out of the editing machine. An audience, in its innocence of all the work you've done, can tell you a lot: they laugh or they don't; they show their impatience with the pace; bewildered, they walk out. It's back to work, profiting by what the public has told you.

Finally, there is a cut that everyone agrees is the final cut . . . the best that can be done; indeed, it may be a delight. Now the personnel list expands to handle all the creative work that must be done before you have a finished picture . . . the music, the sound effects, and the dialogue replacement problems are all treated in chapters Twenty-two and Twenty-three.

Now, at this final cut, comes a creative challenge that the producer shares with the distribution people who have seen the film by now: (1) the name of the picture, (2) the advertising campaign theme, (3) the design and editing of the main-credit titles . . . all related one to the other in terms of selling the picture to that big prospective audience out there, reading their newspaper, watching their TV, and reacting to that new picture's title.

1. The script somehow picked up a name along the creative line that has stuck to it right through production. Now comes a chance to check out its appeal. Try it on friends, your agent, and, sometimes, run an audience survey of a few hundred citizens to see how they react to a short list. The producer can fumble through endless sources of title ideas . . . from the script's dialogue, from somewhere in all the chats about the day's work on the stage (Sexy, it is . . . romantic, it ain't), in the cutting room someone said, "There's never a dull moment." If it's action/adventure, does it have a vital look and sound, and if it's a romantic comedy, is the title itself a small chuckle? (Of course, this problem does not arise if your film is based on a well-known novel or play). One must be open to change because of the number of pictures that have done badly at the box-office just because the public misconstrued its content from its title. (As you know, the most commercial title of all is still unused and available: *Sex And Violence.*)

2. The distribution people will develop the advertising strategy, which may push the title into the public mind, or they may decide to push the star name, or they may headline the content . . . the thrust . . . of the picture.

3. Then the above decisions come to the cutting room gang (producer, director, editor) for the design of the up-front credits . . . that bit of footage when sight and sound get the picture properly started. (Private companies and most film laboratories have experts which the producer may turn to if the title idea is demanding as to art work or optical complications.) That credit sequence can go all the way from the bareness of *Apocalypse Now*—a jungle hillside suddenly goes up in flames and then the letters slowly

appeare . . . .and that's it until the end (although, in its premiere runs, the audience was given a booklet with the list of creative contributors to the picture rather than end credits)—to a recent movie wherein the opening credits went on and on for about three minutes, intermittently mixed in with what amounted to the first sequence of the story: some guys creep down a dark street, there's an all-night diner doing a little business, the guys burst in, the cop car draws up, shots are exchanged, a cop goes down . . . then the final credit (always the director's) and the story was under way without further interruption. (I heartily disapprove of this method of starting a picture, mixing personnel notices with dramatic content.) Almost any variation you can think of between these two extremes have been used at one instance or another. Lately, putting the name up early, after the audience attention has been grabbed, and then putting off personnel lists until the end, has become common . . . and, I think, quite sensible. Another sensible method is to let title music put the audience in the mood while you give them the name of the picture and the people who made it and are to perform in it over a plain or vaguely impressionistic background . . . artwork, black velvet, gray mist, or ? (not over a long shot of the city or the mountain where the picture is to take place; DO NOT give two different types of information at once!)

Producer, get into this title business . . . while respecting the distributor's expertise . . . for your potential audience first learns of your enterprise by its name, then by the impression conveyed by the "advertising look" in their newspapers or TV, then as they get settled in their theater seats, wondering what you are up to.

The editor will stay on throughout the post-production process as the center for coordination of the dialogue-track repair, the music editing, the sound-effects work, the preparation of credit title backgrounds (if they are from the picture, not artwork), the necessary reprints, etc.: post-production housekeeping. And that sounds menial, which is far from the reality of a good editor; true, the cutting room is the functional center of all the mechanics of post-production work, but the creative talents there will bear heavily on the final results artistically. An experienced editor has gone through this process more often than any of us . . . has seen more ways *not* to solve a problem . . . has tested hundreds of little tricks that can get one out of a difficulty. In a pinch, or a quarrel, the producer should rely on that body of experience.

In most television, the editorial process is much simpler because the shorter production time has given rise to fewer camera set-ups, i.e., fewer choices on how to cut a scene together. The director has been forced by time restrictions to pre-cut while shooting . . . choose a single cutting attack on this scene and not shoot several alternate ways of doing it. And, usually, the stories are more simply told. In "The Twilight Zone," most scripts would be basically four or even three major scenes, and the director did *not* provide the co-creators with four ways to cut the scene. But the editor in television has one big added complication: the exact time-frames that the broadcast media demands; a half hour show must be cut to run exactly, let's say (depending on which network and at which time of day it broadcasts), twenty-three-plus minutes . . . with a commercial break designed to fall no later than fourteen minutes after the start of the show. An hour show gets a little more complicated, and a show running two or three hours . . . a little more.

You will have noticed that there is a somewhat different role for the producer to play in post-production than there was during the shooting period. In television, he takes full charge most of the time due to the inaccessibility of the director. In feature production, he drops the reticence that shooting pressures dictated, and joins the creative teams that form up in post-production as a minute-to-minute partner. He should do this firmly and surely, or else some of the goals, ideas, dreams that were in mind long before anyone else came on the picture can be lost.

If the producer and the director are the conductors of this post-production orchestra, then the editor is the concert master; choose him carefully.

22
MUSIC

THE UNDERSCORE

Unless the producer is, himself, a composer or a music/record buff of some depth or an instrumentalist of fine perceptions, he should probably stay out of this area creatively . . . at least until he hears the music on the scoring stage, which, unless he can read music, is the first time he'll really understand the composer's plans. Sure, the composer will have articulated what he is up to, and the producer may have expressed a thought or two, but words just don't do the job for either party in describing a music plan.

Barring the extremes of loud trumpets or banks of violins, which the producer may rightly want in order to shore up weak spots, he would be wise not to set his mind too firmly on what sort of music the picture requires; the director too may have an opinion in this regard . . . he may have heard a certain sort of music in his mind's ear as he worked, but, still . . . HIRE THE BEST AVAILABLE, AFFORDABLE COMPOSER AND LET HIM TELL YOU!

The "best" will be one of those composers who have dealt with your type of film before; and this you will have determined by checking with the half dozen fine composer's agents around any production center. They know what their clients are good at, and will cite credits to prove it to you.

Even with that help, picking a composer is treacherous ground for a producer; their capacities are so hard for anyone but a musician to judge. Their skills aside, their personal response to your picture may vary from personality to personality. Unlike writers and directors, it seems impossible to pin-point their strengths and creative instincts. For one thing, most musicians whom I know are MUSIC from head to foot; that's nine-tenths of what they're interested in. They're not dumb in other quarters, they're just totally consumed with their musical being; all else is diversion. Well, place that sort of pre-occupation on an intelligent person and you're dealing with a genius of a sort.

During "Twilight Zone" days, I was advised in musical matters by the head of CBS music . . . Lud Gluskin . . . who was infallible in selecting composers; the show had wonderfully appropriate music and it was all Gluskin's fault, but I'm not sure that I know how he picked them. I think that composers are less specialized than other artists; I have come to believe that a good one can put the right music behind most any kind of show, be it violent, sentimental, youthful, geriatric.

Early in life, I was impressed with a musicians adaptability; once, in college, I had to arrange the program for a concert to be conducted by the, then-head conductor of the Los Angeles Philharmonic, Otto Klemperer. By a committee majority we wanted the principal rendering of the evening to be Tchaikovsky's *Pathétique*. Mr. Klemperer curled his lip: sentimental nonsense . . . hard to get a discriminating musical mind around. I argued him into it. On show night, the audience and the principal music critic for the Los Angeles Times agreed that Klemperer's version was the best they had ever heard.

Later on, the adaptability of true musical talent was

drilled into me. I met Henry Mancini when I had a hand in the "Peter Gunn" pilot, for which he did the bouncy jazz theme; years later, for a very different kind of show, "The Richard Boone Show" (neither bouncy nor jazzy), I asked Mancini to do a main title theme. He asked, "You want heraldry?" I said, "Yes. Y'know, fanfare." I got as stately and high-status-sounding a one-minute march as one could ask for; beautiful.

So, I have the feeling that a composer who is qualified by some experience is an all-around player . . . any position, any game.

Show this highly creative man your final cut; let the dramatic or comic or violent impact go through his bones. Discuss it, but *lightly*; don't distort his vision with the thought that maybe he should comply with your ideas. Generally, all hands will now go through the picture in a "stop and go" projection session during which the composer will point out, and plan for, those sequences to which he thinks he can contribute. The producer's only comment during this session may be to ask for music under a scene that he thinks is weak . . . needing emotional support from the score.

About now, the budget will get some thought in terms of orchestra size and scoring date; the producer should see to it that there is money for the composer to have at least six weeks to prepare. He will usually conduct the orchestra, but he often turns over some of the arranging to a familiar assistant.

(The composer only plans for the music under main credit titles and end credits after he has composed the thematic approaches to the whole picture; then he re-arranges that music for "front-end emphasis" and "finale tone" according to the footages of each given to him by the editor or title designer.)

The aesthetics of screen music is both written about and lectured upon elsewhere, and better than I can hope to equal. Nevertheless, I have a view of it: it should be sub-sensory; whenever it comes to your attention, it is wrongly composed or out of place. In an action/adventure picture, the trumpets blare to enhance the excitement and there's so much going on in front of your eyes that you don't notice the music, other than to know that you are stirred up as if you were in a gin-fizz blender. If that blast of high volume music is disproportionate to what is going on on the screen (i.e., it's just a shot of a limo putzing down a city street on an evil mission), then the collective mind of the audience is taken away from the story's thread.

Similarly, at the other extreme, when the violins and the flutes lead you down a lovely garden-path of emotion, you only know that the collective effect of story, photography, acting, music, is moving you deeply. As soon as you note the weight of the violin onslaught, things have been overdone.

Music must not compete for audience attention. A strong melodic line under significant dialogue can pull the rug from under the words; the audience ear is listening to the *Blue Danube* instead of "Tell me, son. Why did you come back?"

There are some mechanics involved here. A music cutter will order reprints of scenes to be scored and give timings of them to the composer; he will mark these reprints so that they can be projected at the scoring session, providing a start mark and a mark for when the "cue" must end (this cue information is often conveyed to the conductor via a tape projected onto a small TV monitor at the conductor's podium; tape cues are much quicker to change in an emergency); the music cutter may well mark the cue picture with warnings of key cuts coming up where the conductor must shift to a new tempo or melody.

Finally, comes the day of scoring with orchestra; you hear it, really, for the first time. It is both a mechanical and creative day for the composer; again, in the heat of this costly battle, the producer keeps silent. An important man here is the music mixer who, with dials and sliding volume controls, will reduce the five to twenty microphones scattered selectively (mainly instrument group by instrument group) throughout the orchestra down to the four to six tracks (depending on orchestral complication) that he will hand to the music mixer on the dubbing stage. And he balances these elements, having plotted with the composer about the sound balance wanted. [See page 181 for scoring stage design.]

The composer/conductor has to place a lot of faith in that mixer. Arturo Toscanini, being essentially a primitive man with regard to mechanical and technical matters, would not allow a mixer to have anything to do with what he called "sonority." One microphone just over the maestro's head and "keep your hands off that dial!" Along with forty other fellas, I made the only film that Toscanini ever appeared in, and, believe me, he was hard on technicians. However, he appreciated technical wonders. Up until the time of our little film for the wartime Office of War Information, he had never heard his NBC orchestra on anything but the 1945 state-of-the-art 78 rpm records; when he heard his orchestra on 1945 state-of-the-art variable area sound film, he was ecstatic, wanting to know why his subsequent recordings could not be done this way. I don't know if he ever understood why not.

The next time that music surfaces in this post-production process is in the dubbing room when all the sounds . . . dialogue, effects, music . . . are put together into balance. The composer is there, protecting his score; he has tunnel vision in this regard. "Let's hear the music!" "But we need to hear the dialogue." "Oh, well, the dialogue isn't so hot through here.

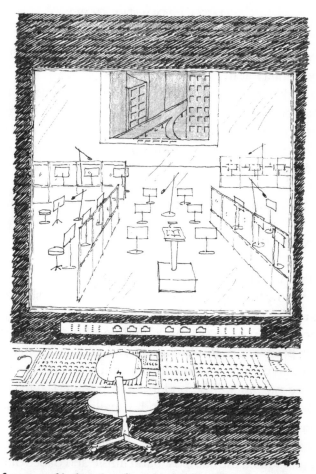

In the foreground is the mixer (imagine him) behind the soundproof glass at his bewildering panel of dials and slide controls by which he can modulate the volume and tonal quality of the orchestral input of the various microphones which have been carefully spotted throughout the orchestra (notice them and also the glass panels that are put up to minimize bleeding of sound from one segment of the orchestra to the other); the mixer has a music score at his left by which he can follow and anticipate events.

There is the conductor (imagine him) at his podium, guided both by the music score on the stand before him (if he's also the composer, he probably doesn't need it) and by the picture on the big screen (sometimes a TV monitor next to his podium) with which the music must synchronize. That picture (or tape) occasionally provides signals in the form of timed dots in the upper right corner of the screen to show the coming—then the arrival—of a change in the musical attitude . . . or of abrupt silence . . . or a softening of the orchestration because of dialogue starting . . . or a quick cut . . . or the sudden arrival of the beautiful leading actress, etc., etc.

Turn up the music." In the next chapter, I cover the producer's responsibility at this point.

Incidentally, all that I've said here also pertains to the music for a television show; the only difference being that the main title music for television was composed some time ago, at pilot time, and that the composer's composing time is reduced to, perhaps, as little as two weeks for a half-hour show . . . four weeks for an hour. Movies-for-Television will take the same mind-set from the producer as do features.

A MUSICAL

I've never produced a musical, although I know in theory how they are made . . . songs and dances shot to pre-recorded playbacks of music composed to fit the story line. Dance rehearsals to playback, and vocal recordings of the songs preparatory to photography. A music director and a dance director aboard in addition to the composer.

The picture will be underscored per the standards and methods mentioned above and, usually, with melodies, or alliterations of them, from the songs.

I would have chosen my director so carefully, and accommodated the composer and music and dance directors so meticulously that I would have little left to do. Unless you are a producer from the musical stage, or a director therefrom, you'd best stay out of the way of a staff of that size and competence . . . it is complicated in ways that most producers never have had occasion to learn. If you are assigned to one, keep silent and learn, then, the next time out . . . take your appointed hold.

The producer's standards in a musical, as to the creative elements other than music, still hold . . . story strength, director skill, handling the performers with sensitive con-sideration, milking the crew for the best in them, etc.

I'll bet a musical is fun!

23
POST-PRODUCTION SOUND

The theorem "Make Sure That The Dialogue Is Clear And Understandable" is about as good a life-raft as any for the average producer to cling to for the ride through the swirling rapids of the complex dubbing process and the preparations thereto. His opinion and capacity to reconcile various professional opinions will be called upon later, when post-production sound has an end-product to judge, but none will be as important as upholding the law of hearable dialogue. Stick to a credo that you can comprehend, then rely on a carefully chosen dubbing crew for the rest of the maze of techniques and machines that these pros know how to handle to best effect.

It is a *maze*! Sound has enjoyed (been encumbered by?) more technical advances through the years than any other element in movie making.

The sound track that they manufacture must be adaptable for use on a six-track magnetic release print (if shot on 35 mm. anamorphic or 65 mm. negative then management will require it for the few 70mm.-equipped theaters around) . . . for use on a four-track optical Dolby Stereo print (really two-track, but matrixed to four???) . . . on a six-track Cinema Digital Sound print (on optical . . . a new boy on the block, not needing 70 mm. stock to contain the six tracks) . . . on four-track (another matrix job) Dolby Stereo Spectral Recording for the few theaters equipped for it (said to enhance both the high and low ends of the recording spectrum for a better all around range) . . . on a mono optical-track for drive-ins and tape for airline in-flight movies.

The most common and widely used of all these is the four-track Dolby Stereo print because most of the theaters in the world can run it . . . through a speaker at left center, one in the center, one at right center, and a few surround horns deep in the theater. Even drive-ins and small theaters with one or two speakers will (under)use it.

Enough of science.

Time-wise, allow about six weeks for music preparation and scoring, dialogue replacement, and sound effects to get ready for dubbing, and about four weeks for the actual pre-dub and dubbing work. (Some complex shows take six to eight weeks.)

As to the "clear and understandable dialogue:" the final dubbed dialogue track will be made up partly of the dialogue recorded on the set during production minus what has been removed from it because it was unintelligible, or was overcome by location noise, or was not performed very well. The removed portions are replaced by what is called ADR . . . Automatic Dialogue Replacement . . . a process by which the player, standing in front of a microphone in a special sound-stage/projection room, is shown the faulty scene, time and again. He is cued by the faulty sound track which he hears in his earphone, and is invited to start, whenever he's got the hang of it, to read that line in the clear of a silent room; he may have to speak the line dozens of times before his reading is in synchronization with the movements of his lips up there on the screen. [See page 185.]

Producer, director, editor, and ADR editor will all be on

The ADR room as described in the accompanying text . . . the mixer in a glass-enclosed booth (imagine him) with a TV monitor that carries both the sight and the sound of the scene being dubbed and a panel of volume and vocal quality controls. Inside, the player is before a silent screen (which helps in achieving lip synchronization) with the faulty sound coming to him through earphones. There is the microphone ready for one reading or a dozen. Incidentally, according to the talents of the player, the loop being corrected will generally run from two or three lines to a half-dozen.

hand. You, the producer, are following up on your demand for clear dialogue, and your ear is just as good as anybody else's; if you don't get it, some in the audience won't either. And the director will be listening for the performance level in the readings; it's not just word replacement, but can be meaning replacement as well.

In the dubbing room this ADR track will be on a separate reel because it may have differences in equalization, in reverberation, and volume levels from the shooting set-track and require rebalancing.

(This ADR can be the dullest of all movie-making processes; the hell of it being that some performers' speech patterns are so habitual and so well-known to themselves that they go through an ADR session in short order and in perfect lip sync, and with the same word meanings and intensity level as the original, while others cannot, for the life of them, remember the rhythms of that day . . . and take forever before all hands are satisfied.)

The final sound-effects tracks (anywhere from two to, maybe, four for a heavy-effects picture, depending a lot on "surrounds" speakers in the theater) emerging from the final dubbing work can easily be the composite result of melding 18 or 20 or 30 or even 100 different tracks per reel. The sound-effects editors have inevitably had an enormous job . . . even on a small parlor, bedroom, and bath comedy. And that track can be tremendously effective. For instance, there was, for mood purposes, a silent, but visual, rain falling at the bedroom window during the love scene. The sound-effects editor finds a good "falling rain" track and puts it in place; it is at one sound level; the effects mixer will probably keep it up in volume while the audience is getting acquainted with the fact that it's raining . . . then pull it down so as to concentrate the ear on the dialogue. A car screeches around a corner and the film cuts to a window on the stage where someone is watching that car; the sound effects editor supplies (probably from the production track itself) a continuum of that screech. Crowd noises have to be added to scenes that were shot in crowds where said crowds were asked to be silent so you could get a clean dialogue track. Interestingly, there are several organized groups of six to ten actors (called "walla" groups) who hire out to sound effects editors and gather under a microphone, gabbling/ whispering/muttering, just like a crowd.

Many of these effects have to be "manufactured" on a special sound-stage called a Foley room. The hero strides through the gravel toward the front door of a house, but this was shot MOS (some early German director said "mit out sound" to signify that he only wanted the action of the coming scene on film; the acronym stuck through the years) to save a sound set-up. So the effects editor strides through his little stretch of Foley-room gravel in sync with the picture, which is running silently before his eyes. There are several kinds of walking surfaces on hand: cement, hardwood, loose rock, tin roof. [See page 188.]

There are sounds that the director or editor want, or that the sound effects-editor throws in for consideration at dubbing time that are not visually cued. For instance, the policeman is tracking the murderer through the dark woods; we hear a lonely dog howl in the distance.

Then there are sounds that are visually called for and damn hard to produce. In *Predator II*, the sound of a growling, animal GIANT: it must be a sound unheard before or an audience won't be impressed; so the sound effects people took twelve big animal growls (elephant, rhino, hippo, lion), ran them slow and then fast onto one track, then recorded that track out-of-phase by 2%—the result was a frightening growl that no one could say he'd ever heard before.

Then there are sounds that get the audience inside of a

The Foley room, named after an inventive sound effects editor, with its mixture of surfaces on which to walk, rap with a hammer, skid, fall, etc. (and there is generally a shallow water tank for dish-washing effects, swimming pool sounds, fishing scenes, etc.). And there is the invisible mixer behind sound-proof glass and control panels ... and a chair for the producer or the vigilant director who should attend these sessions because, being a creative and not merely mechanical processes, they are very important.

character's consciousness—they're helpful but not always mandatory (so a good sound-effects team tackles the opportunity): as an auto-accident victim comes to awareness, his return to clarity could be photographed and understood with just his eyes; but add a little! First a nearby voice, dim; then some footsteps, clearer; then a car run-by, startlingly close; a horn! Eyes open! Better!

These are all technical matters, simplistically described, but necessary to these pages if the producer is to understand the range of the talent that is at his disposal. These sound-effects people could, and would, get the job done without any counsel; but each of them is pleased to accomplish more than a bare, self-evident minimum if suggestions or ideas come up, especially necessary are those that had their birth back when the picture was just shaping up, before the sound effects people were around to hear of the nuances. Part of the drama behind the policeman tracking the murderer through the woods, just referred to, is that he is a big-city boy, used to massive, noisy, siren-laden assistance being at hand when it's needed . . . and here he is in lonely danger out where the only voice you hear is the howl of a distant old hound dog. This is an instance which demonstrates that a sound effect, or complete silence, can contribute as much to the emotional effect of a scene as music. One should always think of that alternative when reaching for an emotional climax: total silence, a telling sound-effect, or music.

Often, there are so many sound effects called for in a reel (as when there might be well over a hundred to get Michael Douglas through five minutes in darkest Tokyo) that there will be a so-called "pre-dub" mixing session during which the multitude of sound effects in hand are brought down to a manageable number of tracks for the sound-effects mixer to handle at the final dubbing session.

There are also complications to the dubbing (mixing) process itself, much less the preparations for it, that are beyond the scope of this book and beyond the producer's need-to-know. To marshal the forces at work and get the best possible finished sound-track, it is enough to know that the dubbing room is manned by three creative professionals who know a lot more than anyone else in the dubbing room about the sounds that will come to the audience from their efforts. Rely on their expertise! The room has a projection screen, with a footage counter at its base (along with, sometimes, a decibel level indicator), facing which sits those three auditory artists at control panels alive with dials and sliding control buttons and volume-indicator lights that rise and fall like a fast thermometer . . . one mixer for each type of track—one for dialogue, one for music, and one for sound effects. Behind them in the booth is not only a picture projector but a dozen or so dummy sound reproducing machines, two or three recorders, all working so that their reels roll forward on the start signal in perfect synchronization . . . and, as needed, can back up—then go forward again—all together. [See page 191.]

Rehearse this behemoth. This is the first exposure the dubbing mixers have had to this picture; they will have fussed around with their dials during the first rehearsal, checking on what they have. They will question the appropriate cutter about what was intended here . . . or there.

Besides balancing all these factors of sound . . . dialogue, music, ambient sounds . . . these clever mixers will take another factor into account: in our usual daily life, our ear and consciousness conveniently silences extraneous sounds when they intrude on what we want to hear . . . what our attention is focussed on. Surely you have had the experience of, let's say, a noisy cocktail party; you have the capacity of reducing all that vocal noise, all that glass clinking, to a nondescript murmur . . . and can hear, clearly, the person

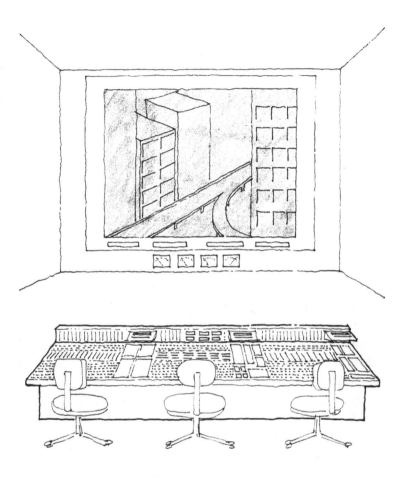

As it says in the text: three mixers on those empty chairs . . . the screen that cues their choices, and the dials and controls by which they "mix" all that is offered them by the complex projection booth behind them. Each cutter (music, sound effects, dialogue) has prepared a cue sheet for his particular mixer that signals the arrival of any sound out of the visually predictable—a sudden music start-up, an off-stage door slam, a voice from the other room.

you are exchanging talk with—you have almost silenced the hundreds of noise sources in that room. But in a theater or in front of a television set, with one to six hi-fi speakers aimed at your ears, you cannot dial out the immaterial; it all comes at you as equal calls upon your attention because it is coming at you from so few sources as compared to the cocktail party analogy. So this team of sound mixers slowly does the natural job for you: the long shot establishes the noise of, let's say, the town meeting . . . loud voices, cars going by, gavels banging; the movie cuts you closer to the principal players . . . and the sound of that hubbub lowers; by the time you get to close-ups, you can hear the conversation just as clearly as you do at the mythical cocktail party . . . only the mixers have done it for you. The town meeting-hall ambiance is still there (you'd be equally disturbed if it were gone altogether), but so subdued that it does not interfere with your comprehension of what is being said.

NOW. The producer should, clearly to all, be the command and communications center (the "clearing house," if you will) for all the people in that dubbing room who want to tell the mixers what to do . . . the composer, the editor, the director, and even the studio head who dropped in for a minute. This is necessary so that the mixers get a single, clear-cut final judgment of what will suit the picture best at every point where there is a question; otherwise, you'll have a horse designed by a committee.

Of course, some reels will go smoothly and quickly. But some reels are a chaos of choices; "Hold the music down in the park scene" . . . "take out the motor noise under the love scene" . . . "I liked the original dialogue reading better than the ADR." Each of those interested parties has a special ax to grind . . . and each *must* be listened to. It takes a knowledgeable judge who didn't direct the picture, compose the music, nor cut it foot-by-foot, to listen, consult with the mixers, the director, the editor, the composer—all pertinent hands—and then to weigh and decide. This is not a matter of a pecking order nor superior intelligence, rather a stout resistance to chaos: smooth administrative control. And the producer must keep his eye on the mixer involved in any difference of opinion . . . for that man knows what can be done and what cannot . . . what balances well for the various sound-system transfers that lie ahead, etc. He is a creative artist himself, as much as the cameraman, let's say. At an impasse, go with his view of the best course of action.

Dubbing is generally a four-week job on most pictures. For, after the work sketched above, the mixers have to make several extra runs with their final results: modify it for simpler systems, modify it for TV, make a "minus-dialogue" track for foreign prints (somebody in Germany will dub the picture into German dialogue, matching lips as best he can, but he will use the music and sound effects unchanged). There are probably other clean-up chores; more than you want to know about . . . for one, sound-track music for the disk and tape market is made with the clear music-track made here, but finished by others, elsewhere.

Television, being less complicated both in content and technical opportunities, goes much faster. We used to mix "The Twilight Zone" in a day. The one-hour long "High Chaparral," with its horses and gunfire, in three days. But technical advances have come to television, too: it broadcasts stereo, and dubbing now takes advantage of that; which means that a Movie-for-Television, looking for a European theatrical market (as some do), has a leg up in preparing its sound track for foreign use.

24
POST-PRODUCTION
LABORATORY

But for the one creative challenge of making a satisfactory answer print and the consequent release prints, this is not an area of expense that can interest the creative producer very much. (A friend of mine and an executive at Paramount, carefully scrutinized the first fifteen prints of the first *The Godfather* to insure high quality for the big city theaters.)

Your lab makes reprints of the cut picture for the music editor, the sound-effects editor, and the dialogue editor. They also manufacture all the optical effects that the editor orders: dissolves, fades, etc. They supply the services of the negative cutter, who, like it says, cuts the negative in a match with the final cut of the workprint.

Then, after dubbing, and with the cut negative in hand, they make the various kinds of prints that meet the needs of the distribution plan: the 70 mm-six track theater, the theater with Cinemascope capacity, the 35 mm Dolby Stereo theater, and the sometimes-very-complicated prints for use on television . . . any feature shot with anamorphic lenses (squeezed image on 35 mm. film . . . on its way to 70 mm. or Cinemascope) must be broadcast in what is called "letter box" composition (the originally shot aspect ratio, resulting in a black strip at the top and bottom of your TV screen) or reprinted in the lab with a pan-and-scan machine by which the film printer moves around the large frame, picking the best composition available; you've seen 'em on the air or on your VCR . . . wondering what happened to the girl for a fleeting moment during the love scene, etc. (the problem is that television is broadcast at old-timey Academy aperture, which is rarely used on any domestic feature picture these days, although many foreign films are shot thus). A careful producer should check at least one of each of these variations on his original.

25
THEN . . .
AFTER THE BALL IS OVER

There are very few comments to be made to guide the creative producer after that day when he delivers the various fine-tuned prints of the picture that today's release patterns demand. Getting into the exhibition/distribution process is, like raising production money up front from banks and investors, a special employment that some producers can pursue profitably . . . and some are just spinning their wheels. In any event, any producer who is enthused about the prospects for his picture will be interested in the ads, the release dates, the theaters . . . all that. To my mind, since that is a very complex, highly professional area, he would be better employed reading material for his next project.

In television, "after the ball is over" is just waiting for the ratings that tell you whether the network is going to stick with you or drop you. The producer's product is being shown in a very different way . . . in very different hands; it's only up before the public once, and that in competition with several other products available at the same time (with a movie they can see the other fella's picture one night and yours the next). Still, luck being willing, you build from week to week, as you cannot with a feature picture. It's a whole different game, played with different dice . . . and just as much out of the producer's hands.

"The Twilight Zone" was in peril of not being renewed, season after season. It was not a hit, rating-wise; *succés d'estime*, yes, but not the sort of series anyone could have predicted would be running thirty years later. Serling's skill as a writer has a lot to do with that . . . also his compassion for the human race as he saw it around him, from day to day. His optimism about the human condition led to stories that made one feel good about the race and its chances for emotional triumph. That, well told, will always sell.

One parting encouragement: all the artists involved in the making of a picture, from stars to the kid who keeps the coffee hot and fresh, work better, indeed at their best, when they realize that they are in a command atmosphere . . . the producer's creation . . . that is knowledgeable, demanding, and appreciative. Learn your job well, and they will rise up to meet you.

Good luck!

THE END . . .

Acknowledgments

I am especially grateful to the following professionals who went out of their way to help me make this book as accurate as possible, as illustrated as needed, as legally clear as demanded. Don Rogers, VP of Technical Operations, Warner's Hollywood; Stephen Burum, director of photography; David Begelman, Gladden Entertainment Corp.; James Glennon, director of photography; Andrew Naud, VP Introvision International; Anne McCauley, set decorator; Robin Peyton, set decorator; Dale Allen Pelton, art director; Alice Kahn, *San Francisco Chronicle* columnist; Joseph Griffith, illustrator; Mike Stroh and John Mann, Storyboards, Inc.; David Stump, director of photography; David Varney, VP in charge of sound, Universal Pictures; Doug Claybourne, producer; Audrey Blaisdell, Head of Set Decorating, Columbia Pictures; Steve Schuster and Scott Anderson, production assistants on *Dead Again*; Aleks Istanbullu, architect; Sue Houghton, animator; Mary Radford, Amblin Entertainment.

The following executives went out of their way to get the legal amenities straight for publication. Carol Bua and Rebecca Herrara of Twentieth Century-Fox; Glen Harris, Cassandra Barbour, and Liz Aschenbrenner of Tri-Star Pictures; Larry McCallister of Paramount Pictures; Judith Singer of Warner Bros., Inc.; Edward Gilbert of ITC. Heidi Schaeffer and Lois Smith of PMK; Evelyn O'Neill of Susan Bymel & Associates.

Then there were Still Department heads who helped considerably. Lou Garcia of Tri-Star; Eliot Chang of MGM; Frank Rodrigues of Universal Pictures; Michael Berman of Paramount; Betty Einbinder of Twentieth Century-Fox; Jess Garcia of Warner Bros., Inc.

Imagine having five highly professional friends who would take the trouble to read a typed manuscript through, study it enough to make helpful criticisms, then like the final result enough for me to quote them on the cover— Richard Donner, Mike Marvin, Charles Fitzsimons, William Finnegan, Francis Coppola. Again, thanks.